The **NO**

TOURISM

'Publishers have created lists of short books that discuss the questions that your average [electoral] candidate will only ever touch if armed with a slogan and a soundbite. Together [such books] hint at a resurgence of the grand educational tradition... Closest to the hot headline issues are *The No-Nonsense Guides*. These target those topics that a large army of voters care about, but that politicos evade. Arguments, figures and documents combine to prove that good journalism is far too important to be left to (most) journalists.'

Boyd Tonkin,
The Independent,
London

About the author
Pamela Nowicka is a journalist, writer and activist. She believes that a better, fairer, more just world is possible for everyone, if we all play our part.

Other titles in the series
The No-Nonsense Guide to Animal Rights
The No-Nonsense Guide to Climate Change
The No-Nonsense Guide to Conflict and Peace
The No-Nonsense Guide to Fair Trade
The No-Nonsense Guide to Globalization
The No-Nonsense Guide to Human Rights
The No-Nonsense Guide to Islam
The No-Nonsense Guide to Science
The No-Nonsense Guide to World History

About the New Internationalist
The **New Internationalist** is an independent not-for-profit publishing co-operative. Our mission is to report on issues of global justice. We publish informative current affairs and popular reference titles, complemented by world food, photography and gift books as well as calendars, diaries, maps and posters – all with a global justice world view.

If you like this *No-Nonsense Guide* you'll also love the **New Internationalist** magazine. Each month it takes a different subject such as *Trade Justice*, *Nuclear Power* or *Iraq*, exploring and explaining the issues in a concise way; the magazine is full of photos, charts and graphs as well as music, film and book reviews, country profiles, interviews and news.

To find out more about the **New Internationalist**, visit our website at
www.newint.org

The NO-NONSENSE GUIDE to

TOURISM

Pamela Nowicka

The No-Nonsense Guide to Tourism
First published in the UK in 2007 by
New Internationalist™ Publications Ltd
Oxford OX4 1BW, UK
www.newint.org
New Internationalist is a registered trade mark.

Cover image: Lorena Ros/Panos

Series editor: Troth Wells
Design by New Internationalist Publications Ltd.

 Printed on recycled paper by T J International Limited, Cornwall, UK
who hold environmental accreditation ISO 14001.

British Library Cataloguing-in-Publication Data.
A catalogue record for this book is available from the British Library.

Library of Congress Cataloguing-in-Publication Data.
A catalogue for this book is available from the Library of Congress.

ISBN 10: 1-904456-60-X
ISBN 13: 978-1-904456-60-5

Foreword

BEING A TOURIST is easy but tourism is complex. This is the essence of Pamela Nowicka's *No-Nonsense Guide to Tourism*. While widely acknowledged as the fastest growing industry today, few question where international tourism's billions of dollars go. Even fewer consider the fact that the 'destinations' they visit are others' homes. *The No-Nonsense Guide to Tourism* tells you what the Lonely Planet does not – that there is more to your holiday than visiting the 'attractions', relishing local cuisines or enjoying a siesta on a hammock by a beach.

Today tourism is being questioned on the basis of who it ought to benefit as against who it currently benefits. People are central to tourism but the 'visited' deserve no less, and in fact more attention, than the tourist. Through vignettes of Shankar the postcard-seller to Raj the guide and Consuela the chambermaid the book intersperses theories of tourism with testimonies of lives of those at 'destinations'. The author's experiences from travel through Asia's popular tourist countries like Bali and India intensify the arguments for increasing responsibility and sustainability in tourism. The book frontally exposes myths about tourism that are built and nurtured by promotion agencies and corporations. Primary among these are claims that tourism promotion is the panacea for the world's social, economic, environmental and even political problems. It questions the motives of those who promote these 'truths', which are used to push tourism on to the policy and development agendas of governments, financial institutions and donors with unseemly haste. It debunks these claims on the grounds that they have almost no basis in research or empirical evidence.

This book is also important because it addresses the tourist within each of us. For no matter how

Foreword

vocally local communities protest, how vehemently
civil society opposes and how ardently governments
strive; tourism will not change if the tourist does not.
This guide speaks to each of us – the average back-
packer, the typical honeymooner, the habitual hiker
and challenges us to think beyond ourselves.

   Equations' work in the last 20 years on democra-
tising tourism leaves us with no doubt that forms,
models, values and politics of tourism need to change.
It requires a reorientation to put livelihoods before
unabated consumerism and leisure, a conscience-
check to ensure that tourism benefits and does not
exploit, and a process of 'democratization' that makes
tourism development inclusive and consultative. This
No-Nonsense Guide places the onus on every tourist,
suggesting a role that they can play in making tourism
more just, equitable and participatory.

The Equations team
Bangalore, India

Established in 1985, Equations is an advocacy and
campaigning organization working towards a vision
of tourism that is equitable, just, non-exploitative and
people-centred. Through networking, research and
advocacy it aims at influencing tourism policy and
practise in India with an unwavering focus on the
question: Who really benefits from tourism?

CONTENTS

Introduction

AS SOMEONE WHO has never particularly been enamored with the concept of traveling, I've ended up doing quite a lot: Australia to visit a friend, then Indonesia, then India. But when talking to guides, small restaurant and shop owners I became aware of another side to the apparent colorful exoticism of their lives.

Heddy, for example, who owned a small restaurant in Samosir in Sumatra, was struggling to give her son the education essential for any kind of a future. The Indonesian smog, Foreign Office travel advisories and the Bali bombs had all decimated tourist numbers, and her income. Most nights when I ate there, I was the only customer.

In India, a waiter in Mahabalipuram invited me to his home to meet his family. Francis wore a shirt and had a large watch. 'Not work, just for looking good' he explained. His shirt cuffs were frayed and his wrists were thin. He had a bad cough. Francis' home, which he shared with his wife and two young children, was a tiny shack. His wife cooked rice and curry. No-one else ate, and his son's eyes were riveted on my food.

Watching the souvenir sellers traipsing up and down beaches, wrapped up to avoid the sun, the work looked hard. The ladies carrying baskets of fruit on their heads had to be helped to lift them up. More hard work.

And beside them the tourists, gleaming with sunscreen, being waited on, frolicking in the waves, enjoying king prawns and cocktails.

I began to feel uncomfortable about the inequalities acted out on the beach every day. But why? At least some local people had jobs, they were earning a living... and everyone knows that life in the Majority World is often harsh.

Today's global travel and tourism industry is huge,

currently worth around $500 billion annua
half the amount of the arms trade – and it
double in the next decade. But it is really o.
tively recently that mass travel has become yet a
consumer essential. And along with this goes a
that tourism inevitably benefits the host country, e
cially poor people.

However many grassroots activists from Sri Lank
in the wake of the tsunami, to Thailand, to Kenya
and India say a different thing: that tourism is
frequently responsible for destroying lives, livelihoods
and cultures and is certainly not, for them, the golden
goose of prosperity it is supposed to be.

For example, control of water and land, access to
beaches, social inequalities and the business practices
of large companies – all part and parcel of the holiday
package – impinge on people's lives. The holiday business is an industry, producing yet another luxury to
be consumed. Governments, business people and local
élites decide where tourist developments will happen,
and how they'll be implemented, with little or no
consultation with local people.

Is there another way of doing tourism, a way in
which it can genuinely benefit the poor and disenfranchised? I hope you agree with me that there is. This
book traces the tourism story, and comes up with some
ideas for change.

Pamela Nowicka
London

**...e likes to go on holiday. The well-earned
...s part of the fabric of Western lifestyle. Yet
...olidaymakers are aware of the impact of this
industry on people, environments and culture.**

√HEN WE TRY to do business with Western people
.hey say "No, no, no. We've just spent $10 going into the
temple and we can't afford more," says Raj, a guide in
South India. 'So we don't get any business.' Raj's words
raise a key issue to do with tourism – who benefits?

According to the United Nations World Tourism
Organization (UNWTO, formerly WTO), in 2004
worldwide earnings from international tourism reached
a new record value of $623 billion (up from $478
billion in 2000; about 10 per cent of global GDP). In
the same year an estimated 763 million people traveled
to a foreign country (698 million in 2000).

Tourism activity is growing at an average annual
rate of 6.5 per cent with the highest rates of growth
in Asia and the Pacific regions. UK organization
Tourism Concern estimates that it is the main money-
earner for one third of 'developing' nations and the
primary source of foreign exchange for 49 of the Least
Developed Countries (LDCs), with 14 of the top 20
long-haul destinations in developing countries.

The growth of this industry has been sustained
and meteoric: in 1950 tourism accounted for a 'mere'
25 million international arrivals; by 2004 it was 800
million and this figure is expected to double by 2015. An
estimated 200 million people work in travel and tourism
(T&T) and according to the UNWTO, 'The substantial
growth of tourism activity clearly marks it as one of
the most remarkable economic and social phenomena
of the last century.' Tourism, it adds, is a human right,
which can help alleviate world poverty and contribute to
international understanding and world peace.

The travel bug

International arrivals have increased from 25 million in 1950 to [...] million in 2004, an average of 6.5 per cent per year. Fastest gr[...] is in Asia and the Pacific, at 13 per cent per year. ■

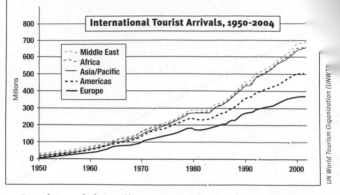

International Tourist Arrivals, 1950-2004

Legend:
- Middle East
- Africa
- Asia/Pacific
- Americas
- Europe

(y-axis: Millions, 0–800; x-axis: 1950–2000)

UN World Tourism Organization (UNWTO)

But how did it all start? And are the remarkable claims made for this sector by its advocates and lobbyists true – or an attempt to conceal the profit motive under a veil of altruism?

In the beginning

For most of human history travel has, for most people, been a necessary evil. Those who traveled further afield than their own neighborhood tended to do so professionally, as soldiers or merchants. Others traveled with their herds. Now travel has been transformed from minority activity to something that is seen as almost a human right – for those from the rich countries. How has this transformation occurred?

A quest lies at the heart of travel: a search for Eldorado – the Land of Gold, or Paradise on Earth. Financial and territorial gain and a sense of something somewhere else that it is impossible to find at home have been the drivers of movement and exploration since people have set out beyond the normal confines of the place and land where they lived. However, one has been convinced about the motives: ...ot much wish well to discoveries, for I am ...afraid they will end in conquest and robbery,' ...ented the writer Samuel Johnson in 1773.

...he Greeks and the Romans traded regularly with ...ia, with caravans traveling the Silk Road to central ...sia, while Roman ships sailed to India using the monsoon winds. The Chinese, too, traveled and traded with what is now Indonesia and further afield.

Who travels?

The Eurocentric worldview is implicit in modern Western travel literature. From the outset, 'we' are traveling to the 'other'. In the same way that, until relatively recently, cultures have tended to view the male as the norm and the female primarily as she relates to the male, non-Europe and its people is given the same relationship to Europe (and later North America). The implications of this 'otherness' continue in the complex set of interactions between

---

'Unfriendly natives'

People who ventured beyond their own territory in ancient times were usually in search of something that would be of direct benefit to them – new land to occupy and cultivate, or resources such as timber, stone or minerals, or any goods they could not obtain at home... Starting with the expedition led by the Egyptian government official Herkhuf in about 2270 BCE there are a surprising number of records of ancient explorers who braved treacherous seas, hostile terrain, wild animals and unfriendly natives [sic] to discover new lands and bring back exotic goods.

Modern geographical texts still unselfconsciously use loaded concepts. Indigenous people are described as 'natives', and are 'friendly' or 'unfriendly'. Trading entrepreneurs are described as 'explorers' and their friendliness or otherwise is never described, although there is often a reference to their bravery. 'The natives' are never described as brave. ■

John Block Friedman and Kristen Mossler Figg, *Trade, Travel and Exploration in the Middle Ages*, an Encyclopedia (Garland Publishing Inc 2000).

---

tourists and their 'hosts' and are especially marked when people from rich countries visit the Majority World, the Global South, or 'Third World'.

The mystic East

According to historian Ronald Fritze: 'Western knowledge of Asia was plagued from its beginnings by a highly inaccurate corpus of information known as the Marvels of the East. According to this body of geographical and cultural lore, India and East Asia were lands full of strange and astonishing peoples, plants, animals, places and things.'[1]

The inaccuracies he referred to resonate with today's holiday brochures. But it is not only travel which is constructed through this sense of the 'other'. The entire relationship between what are now called 'developed' and 'developing' countries, Rich and Poor countries, First and Third World/Majority World, or North and South has remained essentially the same for centuries. In travel literature and in our thoughts about travel and tourism, there continues what author Edward W Said described as '...this flexible positional superiority, which puts the Westerner in a whole series of possible relationships with the Orient without ever losing him [sic] the relative upper hand.' This applies to all those non-European countries and their inhabitants, all those places whose people were, and surprisingly often still are, called natives.

The existence of China and its silk was known by the time of Pliny the Elder in 23-79 CE and there are reports of Romans and Han Chinese trying to establish direct contact between their two cultures, but nothing of substance came of these efforts. Instead, with the decline and fall of the Western Roman Empire, Westerners turned away from the East.

However, with the Crusades in the 11th century, Europeans once again began to engage with China and other Far Eastern lands. The Spanish Jewish

What is tourism?

Benjamin of Tudela's description of his travels during 1166-71 was the first book in Western Europe to mention China or a route to China.

The wishful thinking behind the Prester John legend (see box) highlights a continuing attitude by Europeans to the Majority World. For nearly a thousand years, dominion has been part of the collective psyche, both implicit and explicit. It has been an integral part of Western culture, and forms some of the cultural baggage which Europeans and North Americans take whenever we venture into the Majority World.

The language of domination and acquisition so unselfconsciously and unquestioningly used in accounts of European journeys into non-European countries is fascinating in both its prevalence and consistency: 'Various European explorers, traders and settlers began to venture onto the high seas of the Atlantic Ocean by the end of the 13th century. This geographical expansion was part of an extension of trading activities

---

Prester John

During the era of the Crusades (11th-13th century), a legend arose concerning a powerful Christian ruler whose kingdom was located in Asia. It was hoped that this ruler, who was called Prester John, and his great armies would come to the aid of the beleaguered Crusaders in Palestine and destroy the forces of Islam.

The Letter of Prester John claimed that his kingdom encompassed the Three Indias... Its boundaries were unmeasurable... [it] was a land of milk and honey but it also produced valuable pepper. Its rivers were cornucopias of gold and jewels... [It] housed the Terrestrial Paradise [including] the four rivers of Paradise ... all of which were also filled with gold and precious stones. Near the Terrestrial Paradise was the much-sought-after Fountain of Youth, which some writers claimed accounted for Prester John's apparently extreme longevity...

During the 14th and 15th centuries, as Asia became better known to Europeans as a result of the travels of Marco Polo and the many other Christian diplomats, merchants and missionaries, the location of Prester John's kingdom shifted to Africa, specifically the Christian realm of Ethiopia. ∎

Ronald H Fritze, *New Worlds: The Great Voyages of Discovery 1400 -1600* (Sutton Publishing 2002).

---

that had been taking place for some time.'[1]

Some authorities are more direct about the motives behind voyages of 'exploration'. The historian JH Parry asserts that among the many and complex motives which impelled Europeans, and especially the peoples of the Iberian Peninsula, to venture overseas in the 15th and 16th centuries, two were obvious, universal and admitted: acquisitiveness and religious zeal.[2]

Parry contextualizes the push for new territories and the process. Land and the labor of those who worked on it were the principal sources of wealth. The quickest, most obvious and socially most attractive way of becoming rich was to seize and hold as a fief land already occupied by a diligent and docile peasantry. For a long period Spanish knights and nobles had been accustomed to this process. And in most parts of Europe during the turbulent 14th and 15th centuries, such acquisition of land had often been achieved by means of private war.

However as rulers became stronger, the opportunities for private war decreased. But, for those keen on gaining riches, another way was possible: 'The seizure and exploitation of new land – land either unoccupied or occupied by useless or intractable peoples who could be killed or driven away. Madeira and parts of the Canaries were occupied in this way in the 15th century, respectively by Portuguese and Spanish settlers.'

What is tourism?

'The Native Problem'

Perhaps unburdened by notions of political correctness, Parry lays bare the realities of opening up trade routes in terms which give a fair indication of the exploring Europeans' mindset: 'Precious commodities... might be secured not only by trade, but by more direct methods: by plunder, if they should be found in the possession of people whose religion, or lack of religion, could be made an excuse for attacking them; or by direct exploitation, if sources of supply were discovered in lands either uninhabited, or inhabited only by ignorant savages.'

These dynamics have been played out in centuries of wars and trading practices which are the backdrop to, and contribute to, the current rich world/poor world split. A few centuries ago, spices, gold and wood were on the colonial shopping list. More recently transnational corporations (TNCs) extract oil, gas and minerals from Majority World countries.

And some argue that tourism is as much an extractive industry as any of these, and that its impact on the environment is similar (see box 'Tourism's threats').

Westward Ho!

Returning to exploration, when Christopher Columbus and Vasco da Gama began their respective journeys in the 1490s they were seeking sea-routes to Asia to the spice markets. But Columbus' efforts were halted by the vast land mass (the Americas) that stopped European

---

Tourism's threats

Uncontrolled conventional tourism poses potential threats to many natural areas around the world. It can put enormous pressure on an area and lead to impacts such as soil erosion, increased pollution, discharges into the sea, natural habitat loss, increased pressure on endangered species and heightened vulnerability to forest fires. It often puts a strain on water resources, and can force local populations to compete for the use of critical resources. ■

---

vessels from sailing west to Asia. While this was initially disappointing, 'new opportunities arose for Spain to conquer first Mexico and then Peru. Vast riches would flow into Spain as a result of these acquisitions.'

Vasco da Gama's exploration of a route to India is described in similarly approving terms: 'When da Gama returned to Lisbon from his voyage to India... he opened a world of potentially infinite wealth to King Manuel and the people of Portugal.'[1]

The impact of these activities on the people already living there is described: 'Native American cultures and civilizations suffered conquest and destruction with many tribes becoming extinct.' Portuguese sea commander, Pedro Cabal, who in the 16th century took Brazil for Portugal, found some indigenous people who were 'quite friendly'. But their lack of knowledge about the existence of gold made the land 'relatively worthless in the eyes of the Portuguese'.

Later, on the East African Coast, Cabal and his ships 'encountered grudging hospitality from the Muslim cities... Signs were accumulating that the Muslim merchants of East Africa resented the arrival of Portuguese interlopers and feared the possible unfavorable future consequences for their commerce. The Portuguese further aggravated the situation by openly displaying their crusading attitudes and their assumptions of superiority.'[1]

The process of the 'discovery' of Africa was not helped by the difficult terrain and a 'torrid climate which encouraged disease, to which these explorers often succumbed. Added to the dangers was the threat from hostile tribes – Europeans were sometimes killed.'[3]

The tone of mild dismay about the killing of interlopers bent on ransacking a country for their own benefit is not used to describe the killing of indigenous people.

Discovery and exploration
Later, in 1577, Englishman Francis Drake set out

to sail round the world. Following raids on Spanish vessels – so successful that on the return his ship the Golden Hind was ballasted with gold and silver bullion rather than stones and clinkers – and a three-year trip via California, the Moluccas in Indonesia, and round the Cape of Good Hope, Drake returned to England and a knighthood. His backers realized a return of 5,000 per cent on their investment.[4]

The chain of exploration and exploitation continues to this day with foreign companies siphoning off the wealth from poorer countries, paving the way for rich world domination of poor countries in other ways such as colonization.

Colonization

In the 17th century, the French, English and Dutch established territories in North America, while Holland's powerful navy allowed it to seize many of the Spanish and Portuguese settlements in the East Indies. Fuelled by the intensely competitive and profitable spice trade, the British East India Company was set up in 1599. Within 50 years it had 23 sites across India and extended its trade as far as China, so that by the end of the 17th century it was a major force in international trade.

Wars, colonization and slavery were the order of the day for the next two hundred years. Chartered Trading Companies which were granted monopoly trading rights by their national authorities in specific geographical areas reached the height of their power and influence during the mid-18th century and had become vehicles for European overseas expansion. 'Trading posts and warehouses were established, and from there it was often only a short step to the establishment of formal control over the indigenous population.[5]

Again, the parallels with today's global companies are striking, and in the tourism industry too where local people are incorporated as domestics, waiters and so on. Business has simply reinvented itself, only this time with a smiling face.

The Enlightenment

The Enlightenment thinkers of the 18th century sought a rational framework to lead the world forward from the uncertainty of the Dark Ages, signalling the coming of new attitudes and habits. Greater peace and prosperity, together with cultural shifts which encouraged more outward looking and less parochial attitudes contributed to travel and tourism being seen as beneficial, especially among the more affluent classes. One outcome was the Grand Tour (see box).

The emperor strikes back

Sometimes 'the natives', perhaps due to their 'primitive' attitudes and 'uncertain temperament' (see box 'Australia and the Pacific') saw off the colonial masters in no

---

Australia and the Pacific

From the time of Captain Cook's voyages of discovery in the second half of the 18th century, Australia was open to European exploration and settlement. Within less than a century much of this wild and impressive country – inhabited by primitive people of uncertain temperament – had been explored, surveyed, and mapped, by people who walked, rode on horses or camels, or ventured along mighty rivers in tiny boats to cover the immense distances involved. ■

Shona Grimbly ed, *Atlas of Exploration* (Fitzroy Dearborn 2001).

---

uncertain terms. In the late 18th century, Britain made formal requests to the Chinese Emperor Qianlong to open his country to British trade. Despite a lukewarm response, the British, keen to prevent the Portuguese from becoming too influential in Asia, persisted.

The British envoy, Lord McCartney, met the aged representative of the Manchu dynasty in 1793. The meeting was not a success. McCartney refused to perform the traditional kowtow of respect, which involved lying face down at full length and tapping the head three times on the ground. 'The Chinese imperial court was appalled. Here was a foreigner, a barbarian from the west, refusing to obey the courtesies that all visitors had to respect when allowed the ultimate privilege of meeting the celestial Emperor.'[4]

Holiday time

Later, with the start of the Industrial Revolution in

Emperor Qianlong

Communication from the Chinese Emperor Qianlong to George III of England:

'We, by the Grace of Heaven, Emperor, instruct the King of England to take note. We do not have the slightest need of your country's manufacturers. Therefore, O King, we have commandeered your tribute envoys to return safely home. You, O King, should simply act in conformity with our wishes by strengthening your loyalty and swearing perpetual obedience so as to ensure that your country may share the blessings of peace.' ■

The coming of the holiday

Holidays were transformed in the early years of the Industrial Revolution in most countries. Vast numbers of workers found themselves laboring inhumanely long hours with only irregular bouts of freedom when (to the exasperation of their employers) they simply took time off as it pleased them – to attend a local fair or sporting event... or to maintain the tradition of 'Saint' or 'Blue' Monday, by which they took the day off to recover from the carousing of Sunday. A key event in Britain was the Factory Act of 1850 which obliged textile mills to close at 2 pm on Saturdays: thus was born the 'English week' of five and a half days, which was rapidly copied elsewhere. In some countries, the number of religious holidays ('holy days' originally) was reduced; some were replaced by secular ones, such as 'bank holidays', introduced in 1871.

In Britain, employers took advantage of the annual 'wakes' festivities (religious celebrations commemorating the dedication of the local church) to shut down their factories for maintenance work. Their employees thus found themselves with seven days official (though unpaid) holiday. In the 1870s, several British railway companies and government departments went a step further and gave their clerks a week's paid holiday each year. Free time combined with improved means of transport encouraged leisure. As early as the 1820s, many London clerks and artisans had picked up the habit of taking Sunday steamer trips down the Thames to Gravesend or Margate. By the 1840s the railways were making such excursions increasingly common. In the North of England, the Lancashire and Yorkshire Railway offered cheap Sunday return fares to the inhabitants of the big industrial cities. 'Sea bathing for the working classes', it announced. ∎

Life in the Victorian Age (Reader's Digest, 1993).

the late 18th century, traditional lifestyles in Britain began to break down. The growth of cities and the dislocation of communities led to change in patterns of work and leisure time.

Since Roman times, many towns across Europe had been known for their spas, where mineral-rich waters had a beneficial effect on health. During the 18th century, these fashionable 'watering holes' became places where affluent people would come to 'take the waters', socialize and find suitable marriage partners. In England, towns like Bath and Malvern became resorts. Others were Vichy in France, Baden-Baden in

What is tourism?

Germany and Marienbad (now in the Czech Republic) adding casinos, formal gardens and elegant hotels to their attractions.

However, from the mid-18th century, doctors such as Richard Russell in Brighton and William Hutton in Blackpool, began advocating the therapeutic powers of sea-water to drink and bathe in, and gradually seaside resorts began to supplement and then overtake inland spas.

In a trend which is still being played out globally, seaside resorts grew up from former fishing villages. Deauville, Nice and Biarritz (France), Yalta (Russia), Atlantic City (New Jersey) and Coney Island (New York) were developed as rail links improved.

The explorers

By the mid-19th century, travel abroad had come within the reach of more of the middle classes, especially British and Americans. In yet another precursor to the student year out, it became relatively common for, as writer Nathaniel Hawthorne observed, 'a young American [to] deliberately spend all his resources in an

---

Cook's Tours

In 1841 Thomas Cook negotiated a deal with railway companies to allow 500 teetotal workers to travel at cheap rates to a temperance rally in the British Midlands, and laid the foundations of the modern package holiday.

For the rest of the 1850s he expanded the international side of his business, arranging and leading tours of sightseers to France, Switzerland and Italy. His son expanded the business, introducing more exotic items such as Nile cruises.

Inevitably, more enterprising travelers were scornful of Cook's tourists, one American in 1890 referring to that 'harbor of the intellectually destitute – Cook's nearest office.' But the same observer was also obliged to admit the convenience of such a place – 'where a highly competent and obliging official maps out the whole [holiday], counts the cost, and assures [the travelers] that he will see them safely through the whole adventure'. ■

Life in the Victorian Age (Reader's Digest 1993).

aesthetic peregrination about Europe, returning with pockets nearly empty to begin the world in earnest.'

At the same time, the exploits of travelers like Mary Kingsley and missionary David Livingstone contributed to a cultural climate in which individual travel was both normalized and given a higher profile than previously. By providing role models and exciting 'traveler's tales' in the form of the books and lecture tours, they were able to demonstrate to the potentially traveling public that anyone could do it.

The package tour

One man who made a huge impact on bringing travel to the masses was the former woodworker and temperance campaigner, Thomas Cook. In a trend which has continued until the present day, Cook demonstrated that, using the then new technology of railways, economies of scale could get the general public to move from one place to another in search of new experiences.

Modern tourism

Travel and tourism became increasingly popular in the 20th century, although still largely with wealthy European and North American élites. But with the opening of the skies to civilian air travel, in part propelled by an oil industry keen to push its product, cheap mass travel was born in the latter half of the century, leading to today's boom.

Belgian sportsman Gérard Blitz pioneered the concept of package tourism using army surplus tents in Mallorca in 1950, followed by Club Méditerranée, the first of their all-inclusive holidays in straw-hut villages in Corfu; five years later a ski-village was opened in Switzerland.

At the same time, authors like Gerald Durrell with his atmospheric renditions of family life in Corfu, and Elizabeth David popularizing Mediterranean cookery

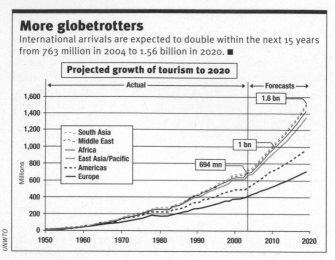

More globetrotters

International arrivals are expected to double within the next 15 years from 763 million in 2004 to 1.56 billion in 2020. ■

Projected growth of tourism to 2020

Legend:
- South Asia
- Middle East
- Africa
- East Asia/Pacific
- Americas
- Europe

UNWTO

for the first time, started to bring Europe into the homes of ordinary people, creating a psychological accessibility which paved the way to physical visits.

As we have seen, modern mass tourism did not just spring fully formed out of the collective consciousness. Apart from its historical roots in trade, exploitation and colonization, its more recent enablers were the rise of consumerism as a way of life in the West, together with the promotion of individualistic gratification as a desirable lifestyle.

Disposable income and the concept of the holiday as an essential element of modern life have often allied with the economic interests of corporations and social and political élites to create a largely unregulated industry whose tentacles reach into all corners of the planet.

For whose benefit?

For many people today, going on holiday means a whip through the internet in search of cheap deals, or winter evenings spent trawling though holiday brochures. It might come as a surprise that such trips are of interest to the UN, international agencies, government departments and business organizations. Not to mention those bastions of free-market liberalization, the IMF and the World Bank.

Tourism has featured on the Doha Trade Agenda of the World Trade Organization. It has spawned a plethora of well-financed agencies to safeguard and bolster the interests of the TNCs who run it. As a major global industry it is surprising that somehow it slips through the net of regulation. Chameleon-like, it takes on the protective coloring of its surroundings. It creates websites, initiatives, partnerships and projects trumpeting its altruistic intent, while on the ground, it does exactly as it pleases.

The industry somehow manages to suggest that world poverty, HIV/AIDS, gender discrimination and world peace are all apparently solvable simply by hopping on a plane, going somewhere else, staying in a hotel and buying a few souvenirs.

According to Geoffrey Lipman, special advisor to UNWTO's Secretary-General, 'We want to fight these common enemies [poverty... one of the primary causes of terrorism]. And in doing so, promote the increase of tourism as a force for job creation, social understanding and poverty alleviation.'

If any other global industrial sector, say petrochemicals, pharmaceuticals, agribusiness, or financial services tried to reinvent itself in this way, the CEOs would be given a stern talking to, told to snap out of it and beam down to Planet Earth pronto. But tourism, with its soft, feelgood product, has somehow slipped the leash of rational discourse. Whether its proponents believe their own hype or have seized on an apparently effective justification for creaming off the human, environmental and cultural resources of the planet, the rhetoric espoused by its movers and shakers has taken on a messianic air.

What is tourism?

The bad news

There is a commonsense perception that tourism economically benefits host communities. Everyone knows how much it costs to go on holiday and it seems logical to assume that as those pounds, dollars and euros leave our pockets they stay in the country where they're spent. But in the smoke and mirrors world of international tourism, all is not as it may seem. From 50 to 95 per cent of money spent by a tourist will leave the country in which it is spent, particularly in the South. This phenomenon is called 'leakage'. It is well-known and well documented throughout the travel and tourism industry.

The views of Mr Annan and the UNWTO are in contrast to those expressed by sister UN organization, UNEP (United Nations Environment Program, see box). Sustainable Living Network's study of tourism 'leakage' in Thailand estimated that 70 per cent of all money spent by tourists ended up leaving Thailand via foreign-owned tour operators, airlines, hotels, imported drinks and food and so on. Estimates for other Third World countries range from 80 per cent in the Caribbean to 40 per cent in India.

Hidden costs

So if the reality of global tourism is that it effectively steals from the poor and cannibalizes scarce resources to give to the rich, why do we all love it so much? And why are not more NGOs campaigning for a more equitable system?

The image of travel and tourism as a sector is key. It's hard to believe that turning golden on sun-soaked beaches or a little light shopping for cheap handcrafted souvenirs can be a bad thing. The beaches are there anyway, local people are hassling us to buy, so clearly they want our business. Hoteliers, waiters and others are smiling happily. We can stuff ourselves with seafood at rock-bottom prices, or fancy ourselves as explorers as we trek, kayak or jet-ski across pristine jungle/white water/blue oceans. It's all good clean fun, no-one gets hurt and everybody's happy. And if there was a problem, governments would get involved to stop it.

This is the Tourism Gospel as spouted by the likes of UNWTO, UNESCO, PATA (Pacific Asian Tourism Association) in conferences, summits and seminars from Madrid to Washington, from Bali to Cancún.

However, there are some dissenting voices around. 'When a transnational tourism corporation floats its shares on the stockmarket, what it is selling is a business based upon human lives, cultures and scarce natural resources,' says the Fair Trade in Tourism Network. 'If the trade practices of a company or the legislation covering international trade create inequalities and an imbalance of power, then even sustainable tourism and ecotourism can be exploitative.'

What is tourism?

Tourism joins the UN

In December 2003, the then World Tourism Organization morphed into the UNWTO, a UN specialized agency, 'as a consequence of the growing importance of tourism and its recognition by the international community'. In April 2006 UNWTO's Madrid headquarters hosted the spring session of the Chief Executives' Board chaired by then UN Secretary-General, Kofi Annan, attended by representatives from the World Bank and the IMF, as well as 30 chiefs of UN Agencies and Programs.

It all seems a bit high-powered and a far cry from flopping around on a sun-lounger, trying not to get too much sand in the sun-lotion while downing an icy beer. But of course tourism is big business.

Industrial tourism

And it is perhaps this disconnect between the innocent holidaymaker having fun and the megabuck realities of environmental, cultural and human-rights impacts, which makes tourism so peculiarly invisible as an issue in the public consciousness. Tourism today is where ethical trading was 10-15 years ago in terms of recognition of what's involved. As a result, most initiatives aimed at regulating it are voluntary and

---

World Travel and Tourism Council

The World Travel and Tourism Council (WTTC), whose executive committee includes CEOs of Marriott International, Whitbread plc, Gulf Air, lastminute.com, Kuoni, British Airways and Visa International, asserts: Tourism can be part of [policy makers'] vision for addressing some of the world's foremost challenges. It brings prosperity to people and places for which few alternatives are available, bridging the gap between the 'haves' and the 'have-nots' whilst protecting our natural, social and cultural heritage.

Travel and Tourism (T&T) generates over 10 per cent of global GDP and accounts for over 200 million jobs. With 4.5 per cent growth forecast per annum for the next 10 years T&T is not only one of the world's largest, but one of its fastest growing industries. ∎

unenforceable, with the predictable result that they are largely ineffective on anything other than the most micro scale.

Governments are largely in thrall to the promises of easy money, treating cultures, populations and eco-systems like a cash-crop for generating foreign-exchange, while for most NGOs, tourism is not yet on the map as an issue, perhaps because its hedonistic connotations disguise its enormous and growing impacts on people, livelihoods, cultures and environments.

For hundreds of millions of holidaymakers from developed countries, a holiday provides a much-needed break from the grind of life in an industrialized consumer culture. And there is no doubt that for many workers in the Global South, tourism provides an income and, in some cases, a lifestyle which would otherwise not be possible. The question is: at what cost? What can the concerned tourist or traveler do to ensure they don't exacerbate the problem? Perhaps tourism can be a force for development, as the next chapter considers.

1 Ronald H Fritze, *New Worlds: The Great Voyages of Discovery, 1400-1600* (Sutton Publishing 2002). **2** JH Parry, *The Age of Reconnaissance – Discovery, Exploration and Settlement 1450-1650* (University of California Press 1963). **3** Shona Grimbly (ed), *Atlas of Exploration* (Fitzroy Dearborn 2001). **4** Michael Lynch, *Teach Yourself the British Empire* (Hodder Headline 2005). **5** Jeremy Black and Roy Porter (eds), *Dictionary of Eighteenth Century History* (Penguin Books 1996).

2 Tourism as 'development'

While proponents of mass tourism talk up the alleged positive impacts, others question whether a concept of 'development' as increased industrialization is relevant, desirable or possible.

THE WORLD TRAVEL and Tourism Council (WTTC) describes itself as 'the forum for global business leaders comprising the presidents, chairs and CEOs of 100 of the world's foremost travel and tourism (T&T) companies'. It believes that T&T can 'help raise living standards and alleviate poverty in undeveloped areas'.

Few would argue that raising living standards and reducing poverty is anything but desirable. What is in question is whether we should be taking the word of global tourism TNCs that this is part of their game plan.

What is 'development'?
Some of us are born developed, others have development thrust upon them. But when highly influential

---

The high price of holidays

UNWTO estimates that around $600 billion is spent on travel and tourism annually. Over one third of deaths – 18 million people a year or 50,000 a day (mainly women and children) – are caused by poverty.

- $1 bn is enough to lift 30 million people out of absolute poverty.
- $1bn is enough to put 20 million children in school.
- $4 bn per year could save 500,000 mothers from dying in childbirth per year.
- $1.4 bn would plug the financing gap for water and sanitation in 14 countries.
- $12 bn would provide anti-retroviral drugs to 75 per cent of the world's HIV-positive people in clinical need by 2008.
- 6 million children could be saved if $5.1 billion in new resources for preventive and therapeutic interventions were provided each year.
- 1.2 billion people live on less than a dollar a day, so $40 billion could lift all of them out of poverty. ■

Shankar's view

Shankar sells postcards and small stone carvings to tourists near a temple complex in Tamil Nadu, South India.

'When I see people like restaurant owners and shop owners doing well I feel stressed. When tourists arrive here, they change money, pay airport tax, pay for hotels, restaurants, taxi drivers, internal flights. Rich people get money but not guides, the mango-seller or coconut-seller. They think we're poor people so they just give us a small amount of money. Westerners spend lots of money on taxis and other stuff, but if we say a small stone carving costs 300 rupees (Rp)/$6 they say they're on a budget and can only afford Rp50/$1. It doesn't seem fair.

If a hotel room costs, say, Rp5,000/$170 a night and they stay five nights, that's Rp25,000/$850. But people like us are earning just Rp200/$4 which goes just on housekeeping expenses so we can't save. Some people get jealous but what can we do?' ∎

WTTC members like IBM, British Airways and US travel and real estate conglomerate, Cendant, tell us that they have moved from the realm of creating increased value for their shareholders to combating world poverty we might be interested to know how and why this sudden volte face occurred. Why has the industry apparently decided to champion the cause of the dispossessed and why, if this is such a high priority, is it determined to do this only on a voluntary and non-enforceable basis?

To most people, 'development' implies a better standard of living for people in Majority World countries: enough food for two good meals a day; clean drinking water, free education and health. The links between this kind of development and 5-star resorts, package holiday enclaves, heliports, marinas, golf courses and shopping malls provided for tourists by TNCs might not be obvious. However, for those struggling to make a living on the fringes of the tourist economy, the relationship is clear.

In whose interest?

People and organizations are divided about whether

Tourism as 'development'

The disappearing dollar

According to Tourism Concern, research by ABTA (Association of British Travel Agents) has shown that 71 per cent of holidaymakers feel that tourism should benefit the people of the destination visited. But for every pound ($2) spent by a tourist, for example on a UK tour operator's all-inclusive holiday in Kenya, only 40p ($1) will remain in the country and only 15p/28¢ of that will be available for importing goods to serve development because of 'leakage' – ie the money leaves the country to pay for importing goods for the tourism industry and debt service. ■

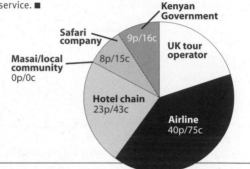

Kenyan Government 9p/16c
Safari company 8p/15c
Masai/local community 0p/0c
Hotel chain 23p/43c
UK tour operator
Airline 40p/75c

Tourism Concern/Leeds DEC

or not tourism actually results in economic and developmental benefits. On the one hand are the grassroots tourism workers, guides and souvenir-sellers, NGOs, and the UK Government's Department for International Development (DFID) who generally agree about the negative impacts of tourism and the mysterious lack of economic benefits trickling down to poorer people. On the other hand are ranged

Corporate view

Addressing poverty is not just an issue of morals. Poverty presents risks to the tourism industry in the form of instability, violence and conflict. At the same time, tourism is growing fastest in poor countries. Enlightened self-interest requires that companies take action to address poverty and as a result minimize risk and open up new opportunities. ■

Dilys Roe, International Institute for Environment and Development, in Corporate Social Leadership in Travel and Tourism, WTTC.

Destructive development

Contrary to the claim that trade liberalization, information technology and the movement of capital and information, labor and goods bring massive profits to people and nations, the poor in the developing world have not experienced them. The economics of tourism is at the root of the many issues that hurt multitudes of people, especially the vulnerable in the tourism sector... The opening of territories owned and occupied by indigenous peoples, farmers, fishing communities have resulted in the forced eviction of communities and the loss of cultural identities. Burial grounds and sacred sites have been converted into luxury resorts and golf courses, cultures are commercialized for entertainment and increasing the profits for the few, all in the name of development. ■

KT Suresh, *Democratizing Tourism!* (Ecumenical Coalition on Tourism 2005).

most governments, the UNWTO, WTTC, the Travel Foundation and T&T vociferously insisting that tourism is a way to combat poverty.

It seems impossible to have two such opposed perceptions of the same subject. But in whose interests do these contradictory understandings work?

No trickle down

According to DFID's Developments magazine, the drive for tourism development can lead to displacement of local and indigenous people, cultural degradation, and the distortion of local economies and social structures. Local people can be socially and economically marginalized by tourism, especially in the all-inclusive package holiday market. When multinationals own every element of the chain – from travel agent to tour operator, airline, hotel and even local ground transportation companies – local people are deprived of a fair share in the profits; indeed, many earn nothing at all.[1]

Vicky Kanyoka, an official for the Conservation, Hotels, Domestic and Allied Workers Union (CHODAWU) in Tanzania agrees: 'While the tourism

Tourism as 'development'

sector is expanding, with an income of $731 million last year [2003], the return to our country's economy is low and the benefit to our workers is about 0.5 per cent of the total industry's income. Workers earn very little and the working conditions are very poor.'

Business as usual
Tourism's inclusion in the General Agreement on Tariffs and Services (GATS) – which aims gradually to remove all barriers to trade in services – has enabled global TNCs to gain a stranglehold on local markets. And despite (or because of) its ubiquity, tourism is not yet on the map as an issue for most NGOs. While for the general public, its hedonistic connotations disguise its enormous and growing impacts. The waiters are smiling, shopkeepers are keen to do business, we're on holiday – and what are the alternatives?

The rhetoric
Jean-Claude Baumgarten, president of the WTTC, states that the global travel and tourism industry 'can help raise living standards by stimulating the growth of infrastructure... providing jobs and training for local people and opportunities for entrepreneurs...' And that it can help alleviate poverty by employing youth and unskilled people in rural areas who have few other opportunities.

However, not everyone agrees. KT Suresh of Bangalore-based NGO Equations notes: 'Experience shows that the tourism industry's purported contributions to employment generation in the local economy are restricted to using cheap labor in low-paying and low-skilled jobs. The problem is acute in developing countries where the common perception is that local people are unskilled and incompetent to manage technical and managerial posts. This relegates them to work at the lowest end of the job chain where basic labor standards are not adhered to.'

The reality

UK NGO ActionAid has researched the impact of tourism in Zanzibar. The situation there presents a striking contrast to the industry's pie-in-the-sky speculation: 'Although tourism development has resulted in the establishment of new employment opportunities on the islands, local people have benefited very little from this. With both direct and indirect employment opportunities, non-locals appear to have taken the biggest slice of the cake. In addition, tourism development appears to have had a negative impact on the livelihoods of local people through its impact on the islands' natural resources... rather than contributing to broad-based and sustainable development, the rapid growth of the tourism industry in Zanzibar has taken place in isolation from the existing economy.'[2]

There is no doubt that, properly managed – so as to prioritize local community involvement and genuine environmental stewardship rather than profit – T&T could help to improve the lives of some people in poor countries. However, it would need a significant shift in the balance of power and a determination by political and business élites to seek out, consult with and implement the results of those consultations with the voiceless and disenfranchised. This needs to be systematic and integrated into the fabric of any potential tourist development, rather than the outmoded, exploitative and profit-driven model currently used by the industry.

Similarly, while there is no doubt that tourism can stimulate the growth of infrastructure, it is another matter entirely to suggest that this will automatically help people out of poverty.

Women

The WTTC believes that tourism will benefit women through employment. But this is not always the case.

Tourism as 'development'

ActionAid comments: 'The tourist industry in Zanzibar has developed into what seems to be an enclave economy, and as such, a large part of the alleged benefits from tourism liberalization has bypassed both local men and women. Rather than being prime beneficiaries, women seem to have lost out to men in the race for the few new opportunities that tourism development has created for poor people. Few women have managed to find employment in hotels and restaurants. Very few women were benefiting from the growth of the tourism industry as suppliers of food, handicrafts, transport services, etc. A woman from Kiwenga village in one of the tourist zones comments, "We have not benefited at all; no women are employed at the hotel. Men sell fish to the hotels. Even though we fish, we cannot sell them to the hotels."'

Sadly, this is also the case elsewhere. Wherever jobs become professionalized, ie paid, it is the men who benefit first.

Research? No thanks

What is worrying about some of the assertions made by the WTTC and others is the lack of hard research into their new favorite subject. They may cast themselves in the role of would-be social justice activists, but have not yet provided the facts and figures to back up their hypotheses. It's no good them hoping that, like a conjuror producing a rabbit from a hat, poverty will be alleviated with a few taps of the magical tourism wand.

Consultation, tailoring programs to the needs of different local communities, and involving unrepresented and marginalized groups – all essential to poverty reduction programs – are not carefully considered.

Regulation? No thanks

And is it unfair to question motives when the industry insists that in the process of 'alleviating poverty', enforcement or regulation are not on the agenda? 'A voluntary approach is crucial,' says the WTTC. 'To take advantage of what business has to offer – entrepreneurship, innovation and management capability – companies must be free to choose how they respond to communities as the competitive market dictates. Attempting to regulate social responsibility would not only be impractical, it would undermine the personal commitment and creativity that fuel it.'

If this is the smoke, then the warm glow associated with holidays in the consumer's mind are the mirrors. Targets and specific measurable results are apparently unnecessary when it comes to helping the poor or conserving the environment. Issues of real sustainability and social justice are diverted by the industry to small-scale 'eco' projects protecting turtle hatcheries, or tree-planting to help the victims of the Southeast Asian tsunami.

Global T&T encourages governments to enact special laws to protect tourists, and can provide services such as a special medical air-lift service to ensure that – unlike local people – tourists get proper medical treatment. It has even created a 10-point Global Code of Conduct for Tourism, but nothing is enforceable, compulsory or is allowed to interfere with the generation of profits.

Instead we are given a pro-poor rhetoric which sounds more like an NGO, and self-promoting 'green' tourism awards. Have these hard-nosed businesspeople suddenly decided that poverty alleviation is vital to their business plans, or is this simply a cynical and opportunistic exploitation of the consumer's lack of knowledge of the industry, coupled with a profound wish that, by making the right noises, business can simply carry on as usual?

Tourism to the rescue
In his speech to the UN World Tourism Organization in New York in 2003, its secretary-general Francesco

Tourism as 'development'

Frangialli addressed the role of tourism in the Least Developed Countries (LDCs): 'Consider the abject situation of the LDCs, with commodities at rock-bottom levels; agriculture eroded by subsidized competition and services non-existent. Yet they all have tourism. And even more importantly with attention from the development community it is an area where they can have genuine comparative advantage and can learn to operate sustainably and profitably.'

Or perhaps not. Opening up an area to tourism can generate more tourist arrivals while simultaneously failing to benefit local people, and in some cases,

---

Local people lose out

In 1986 the Zanzibari Government made tourism central to its overall development policy, inviting 'foreign and private Zanzibari investors to help develop the island's potentially immense tourist sector'. In 10 years the number of tourists doubled. According to the Zanzibar Commission for Tourism this growth has brought tremendous benefits to the people, in both direct and indirect terms, with around 6,000 directly employed and an estimated 37,000 indirectly dependent on tourism for their livelihood.

However, far from spreading the goodness around, tourism development in Zanzibar has resulted in an enclave economy, dependent on foreign capital and non-local labor rather than broad-based development to the benefit of the local population. This is despite the fact that the 1986 Investment Protection Act obliges investors to employ Zanzibaris unless it is strictly necessary to bring in people from abroad.

According to the Zanzibari Government, there are three main reasons why local people have lost out. 'Firstly, foreign investors who come mostly from Italy, the UK and Spain, own 60-70 per cent of all hotels on the islands. They often have experience of running hotels in other East African countries and prefer to bring their own staff, both East African and European, to Zanzibar. Secondly, longer experience with the tourist trade and the existence of better language skills in the northern part of the mainland and other East African countries has resulted in high migration of labor into Zanzibar. A third reason is lack of skills. A large part of the Zanzibari workforce lacks the language and service skills, as well as the professionalism, required to take up employment in the industry. ■

Equal Opps? Action Aid, 2005.

---

undermining their livelihoods. There is no simple equation in which more tourists = better off local communities.

In the same way that the introduction of global agribusiness can undermine the livelihoods of local suppliers, destroy communities and devastate economies, tourism can be negative. But in tourism the links between consumer and supplier are less clear. The tourist assumes that because they are 'abroad' and the hotel staff are 'local', this is where their dollars go. The reality is that, in most instances, it is the shadowy tourism companies that cream off the profits.

Zanzibar is not an isolated case; it is typical of the workings of the industry. All those assumptions we have about travel and tourism helping people in the Majority World appear to be wrong. It just doesn't make sense... or does it?

The problem of 'leakage'

Statistics from UN agencies to NGOs repeatedly show that most of the tourist spend goes out of the host country – 'leakage' – or into the hands of the already wealthy. Like corner shops losing out to supermarkets, small local tourist businesses are unable to compete. However, UNWTO chief Frangialli seems unaware of this: 'When tourists visit poor countries the money they spend goes directly into local economies and communities. Often it helps to support small enterprises, to provide jobs for women and young people, to enhance sanitation and hygiene.'

The Action Aid study on tourism in Zanzibar is representative of a global phenomenon. Everything from food to handcrafts is imported from the mainland or Kenya, so local people lose out. And even when local industries have benefited, as has fishing, results for Zanzibaris have been mixed.

An increase in tourists has driven up the demand for fresh fish and prices have soared. As a result, bigger fishing entrepreneurs have come into the area, displacing smaller ones, with a resulting loss in income. Families have lost an important source of income and nutrition, while a finite natural resource is depleted.

Enter the World Bank

The UNWTO has signed an agreement with the World Bank and is preparing to sign accords with the Regional Development Banks so that they place tourism higher on their agenda. This is why it is encouraging countries to develop tourism as part of their poverty reduction strategies, and the International Civil Aviation Organization to explore ways to put low cost air services into the countries that need them the most.

And, finally, that is why UNWTO has launched the Sustainable Tourism and Environment Project (ST-EP) initiative to put sustainable tourism 'in the service of the fight against poverty and drive new funding, new research and most importantly seed-fund thousands of new model micro projects by 2015 as its contribution to the Millennium Development Goals [UN targets for the provision of basic needs].'

Big ST-EPs

According to Jun Young-Jae, director-general of ST-EP, their projects are 'structured to harness the developmental power of tourism in the fight against world poverty. The objective is for local communities to participate in the entire development process... sustainability is not limited to the economic but also expands to the social and ecological sphere given that the poor are not required to compromise their culture in order to earn a living.'

Mr Jun continues: 'The creation of the ST-EP Foundation was based on the realization that if tourism is to bring about real improvements to the lives of local people and communities... there is a need for a practical framework that can enhance the realization of this goal. It is known that in general terms, tourism can help eradicate poverty, but it is not quite known how these benefits would adequately penetrate the lives of the locals and continue to do so over a period of time. Alleviating poverty is such a giant task and we believe that with this initiative we can contribute modestly and make a difference.'

As of September 2006, the ST-EP initiative will contribute around $700,000 worth of funding which will be divided among six approved projects. Mr Jun's more circumspect and honest appraisal of the relationship between T&T and poverty alleviation flies in the face of the prevailing industry view of its benefits to the poor. The question must be raised: if global T&T already alleviates poverty as it says it does, why is it necessary to create a new agency specifically to do this, and with such a small, unenforceable remit?

There may be a way in which tourism can help towards achieving the Millennium Development Goals but this will not happen by assuming that what's good for TNCs is good for poor communities. Local people need to be involved in tourist development projects from the outset, with meaningful consultation to ensure that money and resources are steered into their priorities, together with recognition by everyone that local priorities may be different from, and at odds with those of governments and TNCs.

Most of all, local communities need to be given the opportunity to say no to tourism and to receive equivalent government and International Financial Institution (IFI) funding and subsidies for other forms of income-generation. So long as IFI funding is targeted at large-scale tourism and related infrastructure projects, local communities will never have the chance for alternative and more sustainable forms of development and income generation.

Tourism and sustainable development

But according to UNWTO 'sustainable development is also an area where tourism is playing an increasingly important role. Our Organization has seen since the UN Rio Earth Summit in 1992 an increasing realization that the only growth which will be acceptable in the long-term will ensure the proper balance of economic, environmental and social benefits... It is people, planet and profits, which must be at the heart of the virtuous sustainability circle. All companies and communities must adopt consistent Agenda 21-based action plans [from the 1992 summit] to progressively reduce environmental impacts at tourism destinations and we shall increasingly work with them and other stakeholders.'

In this brave new world of Orwellian newspeak, tourism is not about grabbing the Majority World's environmental and cultural resources for the benefit of various élites; and has nothing to do with making billons of dollars' profits for businesspeople and shareholders. It has been reinvented, surgically nipped and tucked into a comfortable form for saving the world.

A force for world peace?

The global tourism industry doesn't stop there. It has an even more lofty aim: world peace. In the absence of a firm guiding hand from government, or a reality check from the NGO community, the chief execs of

T&T have seen an opportunity.

People plan their holidays thinking only of a little rest and relaxation; sun, sea, sand and sangria, perhaps a trundle round a museum, art gallery or ancient monument. The more adrenaline-fueled might try their hand at white-water rafting, trekking or visiting a safari park. But most, if not all, might be surprised to discover that they are actually participating in a force for world peace, which was simultaneously eradicating poverty, combating HIV/AIDS, conserving the environment and preserving culture.

If representatives of any other global industry, say, mining, pharmaceuticals or financial services suggested that they would promote world peace or alleviate poverty as part of their business remit, eye brows might be raised. But global T&T is special. Welcome to the wonderful wacky world of the UN World Tourism Organization.

UNWTO in Wonderland

In 2003, UNWTO's Frangialli asserted: 'As regards peace, it is well known that in any post-conflict agreements the very first area the parties choose for normalization of relations is tourism. Furthermore, people-to-people contacts are recognized as constituting the first bridge to cultural understanding... WTO, in its capacity as a UN executing agency since 1976, is today working in dozens of former "crisis areas" to build these human peace bridges – often with support from UNDP or the World Bank. In Rwanda UNWTO is helping to rebuild tourism based on that country's outstanding biodiversity. Having prepared the original Tourism Master Plan for Sri Lanka some years ago, UNWTO is now looking to define new objectives in the context of the peace process.'

Meanwhile, back on earth...

We'd like to believe that what the UNWTO says is

Tourism as 'development'

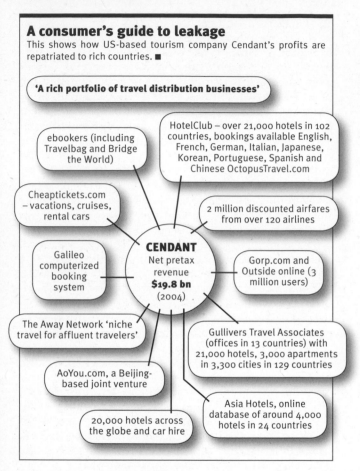

A consumer's guide to leakage

This shows how US-based tourism company Cendant's profits are repatriated to rich countries. ■

'A rich portfolio of travel distribution businesses'

HotelClub – over 21,000 hotels in 102 countries, bookings available English, French, German, Italian, Japanese, Korean, Portuguese, Spanish and Chinese OctopusTravel.com

ebookers (including Travelbag and Bridge the World)

Cheaptickets.com – vacations, cruises, rental cars

2 million discounted airfares from over 120 airlines

Galileo computerized booking system

CENDANT
Net pretax revenue
$19.8 bn
(2004)

Gorp.com and Outside online (3 million users)

The Away Network 'niche travel for affluent travelers'

Gullivers Travel Associates (offices in 13 countries) with 21,000 hotels, 3,000 apartments in 3,300 cities in 129 countries

AoYou.com, a Beijing-based joint venture

Asia Hotels, online database of around 4,000 hotels in 24 countries

20,000 hotels across the globe and car hire

true. Who wouldn't like to be a 'peace bridge' when they went on holiday? The trouble is that tourism is far more complicated than tanning on a beach or visiting ancient monuments would suggest. In a world dominated by businesses and governments promoting a monoculture of consumerism and infinite economic growth, the unwitting tourist on their sun lounger, slathered in sunscreen, has become a foot soldier of the global neoliberal economic agenda.

So, what's surprising about Cendant, an obviously successful, US-based company, extolling its profitability and growth to its shareholders? Its approach of vertical integration is key to the siphoning out of profits from Majority World countries and integral to the non-trickle-down of profits and benefits to local communities.

Vertical integration

When the same company owns the travel agent through whom you book your holiday, the airline that takes you there, the tour operator who organizes your trip, the hotel you stay in and all the electronic systems which allow this process, this is an example of vertical integration, explains Tourism Concern.

With horizontal integration, a TNC which mines in the Amazon may also have stakes in construction, tourism and leisure companies. Large foreign ownership of tourism makes things easier for the tourist, but often means that major economic benefits do not reach the local community.

The reach and depth of Cendant's penetration, both horizontally and vertically into the global travel market – including the less visible 'backroom' booking systems, is striking. This creates economies of scale, tying in revenue streams from smaller subsidiaries, which the consumer may assume to be more independent, and allowing profits to be siphoned back to the US, a graphic demonstration of how 'leakage' occurs (see box).

David and Goliath

The tourism industry looks profitable and joined up because it is – and that means there is little space for the smaller hotelier or travel agent to get a look-in, particularly in the Global South. In the same way that supermarkets drive down prices to farmers and

In the asCendant

While the name of US-based travel conglomerate and WTTC member, Cendant, may not be familiar, its global breadth is typical:

'The emerging part of our business is order-making, which involves our hotel distribution business, online travel agencies, online corporate travel management, and long-haul air travel and travel product consolidators. As an order-maker, we form relationships primarily with the traveling customer, offering them access to our extensive travel inventory... Our global reach enables us to add value to travel suppliers which drive more sales. Order-making is a scale-driven business, fueled by brand and loyalty, with higher sales leading to even greater profitability.

2004 was another year of record results in which we demonstrated continued organic growth and generated $2.2 billion in free cash flow. Net revenues rose 10 per cent to $19.8 billion and pretax income rose 18 per cent to $2.6 billion in 2004.' ■

Cendant 2004 Annual Review.

smallholders and sell standardized products, T&T corporations provide the consumer with the illusion of holiday choice, at the expense of small businesses, communities and the environment.

Is it too much to expect the tourism giants now to invest in genuinely forward-thinking initiatives which promote genuine poverty reduction and self-sufficiency in the poor world? We have seen that supposedly these are now aims of the WTTC. Yet nowhere in Cendant's glossy review, for example, is found a commitment to these. Nor is there a list of successful ways in which they have been achieved and core strategies to continue to extend this process – all of which are there for the company's financial results and strategies. Perhaps this omission is suggestive of how seriously these kinds of claims may be taken.

Cendant is not unusual in this respect, though as a major T&T player, its lapse is as revealing as it is disappointing: it is probably no different from other TNCs in the sector, despite the speak from both UNWTO and the WTTC urging governments to trust

KT Raj, Indian tourist guide

Unlike TNCs worth billions of dollars, individuals trying to scrape a living from tourism are largely left to do it without soft loans, tax breaks, subsidies and the like. In countries without social security systems, the long non-tourist season leaves people struggling to make ends meet. The moneylender charges 5 per cent interest per month. ■

Business development support
- Clothing grant – not available
- Business skills training – not available
- Bookkeeping/accounts training – not available
- PR/marketing skills training – not available
- Soft loans – not available
- Tax breaks/subsidies/business support – not available
- Website presence – none

Income
- Rp50-500* guiding fees per guiding (at client's discretion, approx Rp1,000-4,000 per month)
- Commission (at shop owner's discretion)
- Annual income approx $500-800

*Rp100 = $2/£1

KT Raj net pre tax revenue in 2004 $800

Assets
- Self-taught guiding skills
- Local knowledge
- People and negotiation skills
- Specialist knowledge: history, religious epics (self-taught)
- Spoken English, French, German, Spanish, Japanese, Hindi (self-taught)

Outgoings
- Housekeeping for family: Rp 2,000 – 4,000 per month
- Moneylender debt: Rp 40,000
- Lending fees: Rp 2,000 per month (5%)
- Informal loans from friends: Rp 2,000 per month
- Contingency fund: nil
- Guide's uniform (new rule – not allowed to work without it) Rp 700

Slash and burn tourism

In 2004 Britain's First Choice travel company announced it would cease to operate in the Costa Brava, one of the most popular holiday destinations in Spain. The reason given was 'destination fatigue'. Spain has had its heyday and has fallen out of favor with both the tourist and the tour operators. For over 30 years it was a prime European destination with 47.8 million visitors in 2000. Uncontrolled tourism development has resulted in fishing villages being transformed into huge hotels and villas with, in 2000, over 676,000 rooms available.

Tourism Concern notes that increasing pressure from tour operators for lower prices has meant falling returns for the Spanish tourism industry and consequently little investment. The need for renovation and the ever-changing demands from tourists have not been met; sunny Spain has lost its edge.

Other major operators are moving out of Faliraki in Rhodes and the Canary islands. Tourist migration is set to head to the relatively unspoilt destinations of Turkey, Bulgaria and Croatia. These could well become mass tourist destinations until they too are used up, and the tour operators dump them and move on to a fresh spot. ∎

Based on Tourism Concern Annual Report 2005.

profit-driven TNCs to furnish the miracle of poverty alleviation/development through tourism.

Tourism flight (see box) demonstrates two things: the vulnerability of the sector and all those dependent on it to external factors; and the speed with which a destination is goes from 'unspoilt' to 'popular' to 'spoilt'. If this can happen so quickly within Europe where economic disparities are less than between rich and poor countries, we have to question further the model of development which the T&T industry advocates are seeking to impose on poor and vulnerable communities.

The tourism paradox

One of the strangest things about the industry is how even in places where it has been contained, it still does not necessarily benefit poorer people. For example, one might think that the small island state of the

Maldives, with its palm-fringed beaches, a policy of attracting only 5-star resorts and keeping these away from most of the population on the main island, would be doing quite nicely from tourism. However, according to Tourism Concern, although the sector is the biggest source of income UN statistics show that 30 per cent of Maldivian children under the age of five suffer from malnutrition – similar to sub-Saharan Africa. Fresh fruit and vegetables tend to go directly to the resort islands, bypassing local people on other islands.

Conflict of interest
While the big operators see no conflict of interest between their desire to maximize profits for share-holders and 'alleviate poverty', the reality is apparent when protestors oppose tourist development projects. See the example (in box on page 50) of Bahamian island, Bimini, 50 miles east of Florida.

Tourism as exploitation
The Bimini/WTTC dynamic is not unusual. It represents normal practice in a powerful and largely self-regulated industry sector which calls the shots to governments under the premise of economic development. It is perhaps not surprising that given the conflict of interest between TNCs, fragile environments and local protestors, it is the muscular TNCs that get their own way.

What is perhaps more interesting is the way in which the industry has performed a conjuring trick of influence so that it is allowed to police itself with no legal mandates or penalties to ensure that it follows its own guidelines. So long as governments are in thrall to global institutions like the WTO, World Bank and IMF to generate foreign exchange; and investors care only about the bottom line; and so long as tourism conglomerates are allowed to ride roughshod over the wishes of local communities, the destructive short-termism of such projects will continue in the name of development.

The pattern is the same wherever the tourist footprint sets down, from India to Tanzania or the

The Bimini Bay tale

WTTC member the Hilton Group is part of the controversial Bimini Bay tourism project in the Bahamas. Conrad Hotels, a subsidiary of The Hilton Group, has recently signed a deal with US developer Gerardo Capo to manage the luxury resort. The development has been under dispute for over a decade because of local fears of environmental and social devastation. Below are some of the impacts and opinions.

The site

A variety of ecologically fragile sites: mangroves, pristine habitat, including lagoon systems and sea-grass beds, and coastline which houses endangered species and a shark research station.

The project

The resort will include a vast marina, condos, a golf course and hotel complex.

The impacts

Bulldozing and dredging of irreplaceable habitats. This will devastate the conch, lobster and reef fish on which the locals depend for their sustenance and livelihood. The maintenance of the golf course will require large amounts of pesticides and fertilizer which will run off into the sea and damage the inshore environment, including local coral reefs. Destruction of the mangroves will make Alicetown, the most populated area, vulnerable to flooding and devastation from hurricanes.

WTTC

Under the heading Corporate Social Leadership, the WTTC states that it 'has focused significant resources over the last decade on sustainable development and has been a social and environmental champion for the industry.' In order to meet its new vision, Blueprint for New Tourism, fundamental conditions include:
• Businesses must balance economics with people, culture and environment.
• The industry must expand markets while protecting natural resources, local heritage and lifestyles.

Bahamas to the Gambia. Local people say they're not getting a fair share of the tourism cake.

The 21st-century consumer is waking up to their responsibilities. Human rights, global equity and environmental sustainability are being recognized not as optional extras, but as fundamental to global equity and justice. When, as tourists, we come face to

---

• It must create locally driven processes for continuous stakeholder consultation.

The Hilton Group

It has published a commitment to social and environmental responsibilities. Its core values include the statement: 'At Hilton group, we strive for high standards of performance and advocate socially and environmentally responsible business practice throughout our global operations.'

Tourism Concern

Local protests have taken place in front of the multimillion dollar project. It promised a primary school, and said that the project would be environmentally friendly. These promises have failed to materialize. The tourism complex already restricts beach access for locals whilst using local water supplies, resulting in water supplies to the community being frequently turned off.

Bimini Biological Field Station

'In the last few days alone they have removed hundreds of meters of mangroves from the shoreline along the south-western region of the lagoon.'

WTTC supremo, Jean-Claude Baumgarten

New Tourism... looks beyond short-term considerations. It focuses on benefits not only for people who travel, but for people from the communities they visit, and for their respective natural, social and cultural environments.

Local Biminians

Reports from conservation groups and eyewitnesses continue to contradict assertions by The Capo Group that the environmental and social impacts of the development can be contained. Local community groups are still protesting about the lack of consultation and broken promises.

Raj, a guide

Before we had a quiet life, and a very happy life. We could see natural things, but now there's more development. UNESCO spent money on the government and monuments, but ordinary people don't get anything.

They've destroyed beautiful things on the Mountain. Before there weren't any fences but about three years ago they suddenly put up iron railings and barbed wire fences. Nobody told us this would happen: one minute it was normal, the next fences were everywhere.

The Government wants to get more money here [at the Mountain] like they've done at the Shore Temple. We used to be able to sit and relax in the garden outside it in the evening but now it's all been fenced off so we can't. All the beauty is destroyed.

So what happens to all the money from the Westerners? It's $10 a person to see the Shore Temple, Five Rathas. It's a lot. But this money all goes to the Government and they don't invest in local people and businesses. ■

face with the impacts of a global economic hegemony which has been set up to protect and entrench our own, often profligate lifestyle at the expense of those for whom even clean drinking water and enough to eat are distant dreams, it is time to question our own part in this equation and perhaps to say enough is enough. The next chapter looks at us, the tourists.

1 Richard Hammond, 'The Good Tourist Guide', *Developments* DFID, Issue 27, Third Quarter, 2005. **2** Sunitha Rangaswami, Birgit la Cour Masden, Matthew Lockwood, *Equal Opps?*, Action Aid 2004.

3 Inside the tourist

When people talk about holidays they think about cost, where they want to go and what clothes they'll need. But why do we need holidays?

IN THE COZY rhetoric that surrounds tourism, holidaymakers focus on the pleasurable and 'fun' aspects of their trip. But as we have seen, the construct which is the modern holiday is part of a complex business process of global interactions in which the desires of a minority of consumers are prioritized over the needs of the majority of hosts. The situation is particularly acute when tourists from rich countries visit the Majority World.

To have traveled confers cachet. To describe someone as 'well traveled' is a compliment implying a certain gutsy sophistication. The 'Gap' year out for students has become a rite of passage for middle-class youths keen to 'broaden their horizons' before knuckling down to college. And we aspire to be 'travelers' whilst a 'tourist' is seen as being more part of the herd and therefore less desirable. But what's the difference and why does it matter?

Westerners are increasingly bowed by the pressures of industrial consumer culture, with its 24/7 demands of work to buy pleasure, status and sense of identity. We want our holidays to enable us to discover that

---

Holidays in the sun

International arrivals have increased by an average rate of 4.2 per cent between 1990 and 2005... which has led the UN World Tourism Organization to predict that by 2020 tourist arrivals around the world should reach 1.6 billion. The growth forecast is even more spectacular in the case of Asia and the Pacific where international arrivals are expected to leap almost fourfold from 111 million in 2000 to 417 million in 2020. Asia has already overtaken the Americas – in 2002 – to become the second most visited region in the world. ■

missing part of ourselves, the part we give up in exchange for the benefits of living in the richest countries in the world.

Why holidays?

There is a mystery at the heart of tourism, and it is concealed under the guise of sound common sense, ie everyone needs a break. But why?

Holidays are constructed as a necessity by Western consumer culture. They are it seems an essential and unquestioned part of The Good Life. Indeed, so vital are these 'breaks' from our normal lives, that the smallest hint that the holiday ethos is at best questionable and at worst, contributing to the destruction of the very places the holidaymaker wants to experience, is treated with the kind of shock-horror that an alcoholic might experience on discovering that the last of the gin had been replaced with tap-water.

Does this give a clue to the real state of affairs, in which increasing numbers of us have effectively become holiday junkies, craving our next away-from-it-all fix of travel in order to endure the soul-destroying reality of a culture in which the twin gods of money and hedonism have become the new spiritual dogmas? If this seems far-fetched, just reflect for a moment.

As tourists and travelers we need to examine our own, often addictive, relationship with travel. Some people like to drive to relax, some will simply go for a stroll. These are the same impulses – the need to relax – but have very different impacts. It's similar with

Desire, motivation, responsibility

However one defines, describes or analyses tourism, it is the tourist that remains at the heart of the matter. It is the action of a tourist [contacting] the travel agent that triggers the complex set of mechanisms and impacts that comprise tourism. ∎

Peter M Burns, *An Introduction to Tourism and Anthropology* (Routledge 1999).

Original Travel

Managing director of Original Travel (OT), Nick Newbury, believes he has spotted a gap in the market for a 'high-end, short break operator'. 'For most people, the two week bucket-and-spade holiday along with a week's skiing no longer feels enough. People are trying to squeeze more holiday into less time.'

Options available from OT include a 4-day luxury kayak and lodge-based safari around the Zambezi river in Zambia (from $2,600/£1,375 per person) or a weekend learning the basics of bobsleighing from former Olympic competitors (from $1,300/£690 a person).

'Over the years British holidaymakers have moved from packages to villas to more activity based holidays. More recently they've developed a taste for braggability and pampering,' says Newbury.

He talks of some 'crazy bookings'. 'We've sold trips to the North Pole and altitude training in the Atlas mountains to people trying to cut their London marathon times,' he says. 'One single booking was worth $44,000/£23,000. It all comes down to an original slant on travel'.

Suddenly the long weekend planned in Rome no longer feels so glamorous. ■

Marketing, 20 October 2004.

holidays. The simple desire for rest and relaxation, perhaps with a change of scene, is fairly straightforward. But modern holidays have taken on a peculiar experiential identity, and become as much linked to the kind of person we believe we are as the clothes we wear or the newspaper we read. They have become a lifestyle statement, branding us as the kind of person we aspire to be.

What is a holiday?

So what do we want from a holiday? Sand, sea, sun? A bit of culture? Glamor? 'Braggability'? Status-enhancing tales of more-intrepid-than-thou-ness? Different

Sunshine and elephants

I hardly remember what my expectations of India were. They must have involved a lot of sunshine and probably elephants. People sitting on elephants. ■

David Tomory, *A Season in Heaven* (Thorsons/HarperCollins 1996).

food perhaps, although judging by menus from the Spanish Costas to the beach restaurants of Goa, fish and chips, burgers, Coke and 'tea like Mum makes it' retain a certain compulsive popularity. We want it to be different enough so we know it's 'away', yet familiar enough that we don't feel out of our depth. Safe but exotic. And not too challenging.

While it seems reasonable that when we have worked hard we need to play hard, the particular status which has been assigned to holidays in industrial consumer culture suggests that something bigger and more interesting is going on when we make the decision to travel. For many, a holiday has become an opportunity to reinvent ourselves. Decked out in our holiday clothes, we can swap our real-life identities as wage slave, city slicker, or call center operative for something larger, funkier, and altogether more colorful: we rediscover the real us. Or maybe that's just the story conjured up by the marketing departments of travel companies, airlines and tourism boards, who've turned a simple desire for a break from routine to yet another 'need'.

Hype to reality

The colonial impulse has also been reinvented in marketing hype, to promote one of the world's biggest industries. It's another way for the conquistador mentality of TNCs in the service of 'market-driven' rationales to sell more oil, displace the poor from their ancestral lands, and in the process make enormous profits, while bolstering the neoliberal agenda (see chapter 5).

In the current discourse around holidays, we are encouraged to believe in the doctrine of 'more and better holidays' as though it's integral to our wellbeing. Although as recently as 10 years ago, trips abroad were far fewer and less part of individual identity and the cultural landscape, we now find ourselves believing that a break is our birthright. Holidays, and particularly exotic ones, are seen not as an extension of the colonial raison d'étre but as harmless and restorative fun.

Holiday literature abounds with aspirational references to 'colonial' this or that in an approving way. In this reworking of the invader mythos, the natives are always smiling. They have to. Their jobs and livelihoods are on the line.

Who are the tourists?
According to UNWTO, in 1998 up to 80 per cent of all international travel (measured by volume) was made by nationals of just 20 countries. Though arguably, if the need for a relaxing break was the main determinant of holidaymaking, it would be the workers in rice paddies, stone quarries and garment sweatshops from the Global South who would be sunning themselves on beaches, partying in bars and getting their cultural rocks off at World Heritage Sites.

Of course many can't afford holidays. But they would if they could... and no doubt the call-center operatives in India will be tourists too. Look at the new middle classes of India and China.

But most tourists are recreational refugees from rich countries. Unlike the 'economic' refugees from Majority World countries, who brave stormy seas in ramshackle boats, or curl up in the wheel-bays of a jumbo jet and freeze to death in search of a job, the tourist is feted and welcomed. They will not be frog-marched to a detention center, incarcerated without trial and re-exported back home asap. It's a simple equation: money + travel = good. No money + travel = bad.

Why travel?
The subtext is that 'we', ie mainly people in the rich world, owe it to ourselves to take a break. We deserve

it. And in that simple notion of the primacy of individual wish-fulfillment over anything else lies the success of the leviathan of the global consumer industry: travel and tourism.

Travel in the sense of holidaymaking (quite distinct from the travel of, say, refugees, or economic migrants) is 'a fundamental human right... almost a human need' according to Ho Kwon Ping, Executive Chairman of the Banyan Tree Group addressing a Pacific Asia Travel Association (PATA) conference in April 2006. The skew that is rarely acknowledged is that this so-called 'human right', like quite a lot of others – clean drinking water, decent medical care, enough to eat – really only applies to those of us fortunate enough to have been born in a wealthy country.

Discriminatory tourism

Most people will never have the opportunity to be holidaymakers as Westerners are – although pilgrimages and other cultural events do bring some time out for many people in the Global South. But for most, their role in the tourist equation will be as picturesque

---

Buying freedom

'The notion of holidays as a means of purchasing that otherwise intangible and much-loved – particularly by advertisers – concept of freedom, is common.

In the urban, post-industrial environment that generates most of the world's tourists, part of that world is a disconnection with nature and spirituality, the abiding myth of such an existence is that of freedom. It is travel and tourism that keeps this particular myth alive and continues with the idea that travel is, as the US Travel Administration claims, "The Perfect Freedom".' ■

Peter M Burns, *An Introduction to Tourism and Anthropology* (Routledge 1999).

'At the point of leaving home with a small bag and hair down to here, if I expected anything of India, it was freedom.' ■

David Tomory, *A Season in Heaven* (Thorsons/HarperCollins 1996).

---

scenic and cultural extras, whose images will be used, sold and marketed, with no form of payment or even an acknowledgement. Those cheerful, often female, often young faces, colorfully decked out in 'traditional' clothing, nameless and attractive, like a sunset over the ocean or exotic wildlife, that stare out from brochures and postcards across the world.

Someone from the Majority World who might find the resources to visit Europe and the US will not simply be able to pop into the nearest embassy, fill in a form, hand over some cash and be issued with a visa. Instead they will be called to an interview, interrogated, be required to produce bank statements, letters from sponsors and generally expected to speak English.

Generally, despite this bureaucratic rigmarole, they will be refused a visa. If Northern consumers were subjected to this kind of harassment and essentially racial and economic discrimination, there would be an outcry. But this one rule for them, another completely different rule for us, merely highlights the lie of 'global' tourism. Tourism is just for the rich, ideally white.

Not in the guidebook

Part of the magic of going away is that we willingly submit to a special form of enchantment. In our media-savvy age of 24/7 communication, we manage

Guilty or not?

I was a guidebook writer for Footprint. I have felt massively guilty on holiday. I do my best to go to local businesses and I don't think people should go to tribal villages... I think I've got remnants of colonial guilt or something... I even feel guilty about the behavior of fellow travelers in Bali – taking E's, stripping off – all that in a place where people are so conservative. – Jasmine Saville, Wales. ∎

In Focus, Summer 2005, Tourism Concern.

to remain surprisingly blinkered about realities on the ground in the tourist destinations, particularly in the Majority World.

Whether it's the level of poverty, oppressive regimes, or lack of basic medical facilities, these remain invisible in the promotional brochures. We may spend hours surfing the net for the best deal, but only a few will research the living conditions of the local people living in the holiday zone we intend to visit. Brochures remain silent on maternal mortality rates, literacy rates and lack of clean water and sanitation.

Another way

We could question our holiday providers about their ethical credentials. We could write to the media arms of travel conglomerates otherwise known as the travel pages and press, demanding stories on the impact of tourism in host countries and communities. We could lobby governments and NGOs to take up these issues as a matter of urgency (see chapter 7).

My life in travel

Q: What have you learnt from your travels?
A: I used to get to the airport check-in desk with minutes to spare but I've learnt the hard way after a few near misses that there are many benefits of an early check-in. I also love shopping there. – Jodie Kidd, fashion model. ∎

The Independent, 1 July 2006.

Generating tourism

Leisure refugees from industrial consumer cultures seek to find the 'unspoiled', which leads to 'development'...or spoiling? ∎

The anthropology of tourism

the generating system: an internally generated outpouring of tourists

- location boundaries
- 'exhausted' citizens who need to 'escape' and be restored
- need to annex externally located places of recreation
- sub-system of travel intermediaries and suppliers

zones of mutual interdependence

the generating system needs to ensure the well-being of the receiving system: it is these 're-creative satellites' that contribute to the social and psychological well-being of the generating regions.

Requires financial involvement beyond direct expenditure by tourists or investment by firms

- within its own boundaries, facilities 'play' and non-ordinary behaviors
- generating countries' (residual in tourists), the general culture of tourists, and everyday local culture come together to create a synthesised culture

the receiving system which subsumes an inpouring of tourists

After κεπri in Witt and Moutinho /Peter M Berns, An Introduction to Tourism and Anthropology, Routledge, 1999.

Wants

Perhaps one of the most defining elements of industrial consumerism is the sense of 'want', translated into 'need' and interpreted as entitlement, epitomized in the cosmetics advertising catchline: 'Because I'm worth it'. However, in the mega marketplace of global tourism this tends to mean in practice, 'Because I'm worth it – but you're not.' This point about worth is illustrated by very basic differences, for example the fact that the tourist stays in a comfortable hotel, with bed, sheets, fan or a/c, shower, running water and a balcony, while the staff may sleep on the floor, get water from a standpipe and struggle to get by on tips.

Inside the tourist

Desperately seeking the dream

As inhabitants of industrial consumer culture, a number of 'givens' are drummed into us from birth: the primacy of individual desire; the importance of celebrities as role models, and that buying stuff will make us happy. In varying degrees, some of us relate to people and experiences as consumables, whilst being aware that this may be how other people relate to us.

Life in the developed world can leave its inhabitants with an emotional and experiential vacuum. Perhaps we feel a sense of disappointment as we struggle to assert what we may suspect is a fairly banal life at odds with the glamorous, wealthy media visions we are encouraged to admire. Social relationships are reconstructed as the electronic pulses of emails and texts; 'community' can become an affiliation of special-interest groups, business, gay, development, and so on. While for many, spirituality is translated as worshiping at the consumer cathedrals of shopping malls.

And yet we retain a part of our soul or psyche which looks for something more open-air and elemental. We look for vistas stretching to the horizon, space and 'nature'. And that innocent urge becomes transformed into the consumerfest which is the modern holiday.

Value for money

In this global merry-go-round, the Western tourist – particularly when traveling to poor countries – can experience at first hand the benefits of an unfair global trade system skewed relentlessly in favor of their own rich nations. Average people from Europe, Australasia and North America find themselves suddenly 'rich' when traveling in the Global South, which adds to the luxuriousness. It's a microcosm of global inequality, often with an added frisson of guilt that yet again we rich are in some way exploiting the poor. But this is mitigated by a belief that perhaps tourism has helped local people. For example, they may be hotel staff and barely getting by without the largesse of our tips, but at least they've got a job and surely it's better than working in the paddy fields.

As for those local people who do engage with tourism, they must deal with the situation as best they can. So the tourist is forced to contend with 'annoying' hawkers, 'dishonest' touts, 'cheating' shopkeepers and a range of uncertain interactions, designed, apparently, to separate the tourist from his or her cash.

Hidden costs
Another aspect of the impact of holidaymaking is its seasonality. This means that resort populations expand to many times their normal size during the season, with a knock-on effect on both the physical and social structures of destinations.

The seasonal roller-coaster
Seasonal peaks and lows in tourism arrivals translate into a boom or bust situation on the ground, leaving the poorest struggling to manage their finances in the long 'off' season.

For those who research the subject, more unpalatable possibilities become clear. Professor Peter Burns, director of the Centre for Tourism Policy Studies at Brighton University, observes that it has been argued that an element of cultural imperialism is an integral part of tourism, particularly tourism to the South because of the inequalities enshrined in the global socio-economic system.

Rituals of renewal
Cultural anthropologists argue that the modern holiday has many of the aspects of a religious ritual, particularly in the phenomenon of cultural inversion, in which the meanings and rules of ordinary behavior are suspended or turned on their heads.

The dark side of tourism

Dennison Nash has written extensively about tourism from a social science perspective. He suggests that the following are key elements in the host/tourist dynamic:

- Analysis of tourist development should not take place without reference to the productive systems that generate i) sufficient surplus to enable tourism and ii) tourists themselves
- This sets up a degree of control by the generating region over the receiving region [which makes] tourism a form of imperialism
- This relationship is totally geared towards supplying whatever the tourists want including that which may not 'naturally' or 'traditionally' be found such as fast food, air conditioning, swimming pools and imported food or beverages: a supporting infrastructure is thus developed.
- Transactions with local people are inherently unequal and this inequality frames the relationship between 'hosts' and 'guests'
There are often economic disparities between hosts and guests, which, like colonialism, can engender feelings of superiority among the incomers. 'People who treat others as objects are less likely to be controlled by the restraints of personal involvement and will feel freer to act in terms of their own self-interest'
- A tourism system may develop (especially within countries with a very limited economic base) which may subsume the general economy into a service economy geared towards meeting the needs of transient, leisured strangers and their sponsors. ■

Peter M Burns, *An Introduction to Tourism and Anthropology* (Routledge 1999).

Other components of ritual, for example the putting aside of the normal rules of life and society, limited duration of the event and unique social relations can all be found in the holiday experience.

If holidays are the new pilgrimage, increasingly holidaymakers are becoming missionaries of hedonism. Preaching the gospel of industrial consumerism by thought, word and deed, they influence by example. Their regalia are MP3 players and designer clothes, and their temples are the internet cafés.

It could be different. We could visit other countries, particularly in the Majority World, as a means of genuinely learning about other ways of living, thinking and prioritizing. We would remove our sunglasses of superiority and engage with, listen to and learn from people with a different point of view. Instead of a parasitic holiday relationship we could enter into something more symbiotic, more genuinely reciprocal and interactive. But in order to do this we would need to be genuinely curious, empathetic and humble in our dealings with local people (see chapter 7).

Converting dreams

As every western consumer knows, there's an easy way of turning dreams to reality – just add money. Forget coming face to face with global inequality and social injustice, our holiday hats are handily equipped

Tourism as consumption
In the same way that consumers buy cars, white goods, clothes or any of the other consumer offerings available, they are now able to buy experience, culture and relaxation. ∎

industry
strategic alliances 'unpackaged' holidays, employee empowerment. 'mass-customization', yield management, performance and process evaluation, TQM

consumers
fickle, value-conscious, ethics conscious? high expectations, changing demographic profiles, litigious

globalization
strengthening of the multinational, globalized competition, cultural homogenization? tripolarity of power

Changing nature of tourism

politics
trade policies, policy and planning: regulation vs. self-regulation, incentives, building a dynamic private sector

technologies
compatibility, emergence of an 'information intensive' industry, increased access for some

competition
quality-driven, database-marketing, shift from cost-oriented pricing to psychological pricing

Peter M Burns, An Introduction to Tourism and Anthropology, Routledge, 1999.

A 'code of ethics' for the tourist

- Travel in a spirit of humility and with a genuine desire to learn about the people of your host country.
- Be sensitively aware of the feelings of other people, preventing what might be offensive behavior on your part...
- Cultivate the habit of listening and observing, rather than merely hearing and seeing.
- Instead of looking for that beach paradise, discover the enrichment of seeing a different way of life through other eyes. ■

www.ecotonline.org/campaigns

---

with blinkers, so we can just party on down.

In the post-modern world we have TV, virtual reality games and anti-social behavior, but 24/7 society can be exhausting, so we have to get away from it all. Tens of thousands of people may be facing starvation and inhuman living conditions in refugee camps, cities and villages throughout the 'developing' world, but we'll jet over the slums and fly across the favelas for our holiday in the sun. We hypnotize ourselves to believe there's nothing we can do to substantially

---

Raj, a guide

Raj sits on a rocky outcrop of what locals call 'The Mountain', overlooking the small town and tourist enclave of Mamallapuram, in south India. He is smartly dressed in trousers and a long-sleeved shirt rolled to his elbows, modeled after his film hero Vijay. From time to time he deflects local hawkers approaching to sell postcards and other souvenirs. 'Western people think they're very great, very clever, boasting about how they are never cheated. They'd think they'd got a fantastic deal, but really it was fantastic for us!' He beams. 'There are tons of ways to separate tourists from their money.

'We have a talent. Our "trick" is to speak to them nicely. "How are you? Which country are you from?" We'd be like a nice friend; help them, get them water, postcards, take them to the post-office, internet café, show them our culture. We don't try to cheat them but we just need to get as much money as we can from them to live and pay for everything.' ■

---

change a system that gifts inhabitants of rich countries with lifestyles of excess, while, according to the recent MakePovertyHistory campaign, 50,000 people die every day of poverty-related causes.

The tourist journey

When a tourist steps off the plane, she or he is instantly transformed from Joanne or John Doe, normal, everyday and invisible, into a 'Madam' or 'Sir', a person of power and status. We will be smiled at, welcomed into shops and restaurants like a long-lost relative, and generally very much made to feel like a person of power and consequence. We will be noticed and made to feel important. Who could resist such seductive overtures? We are special.

Complicity

But it's not our film star looks or charisma that have brought us all this attention, it's the power of our dollars, euros and pounds. Fabulous Forex – foreign exchange – those desirable 'hard' currencies for which many Majority World élites will happily sacrifice their own people, cultures and environments. But why should our spending power have so suddenly and gratifyingly multiplied 10 times?

The answer to this conundrum is not hard to find, for tourism allows us to experience our own personal microcosm of the global economic reality. The theory of trade rules and global inequity is available

---

Blind eye

It seems that holidays can be unfair, everyone is getting a raw deal and it's not right. These people are so poor, there's just no need. It makes you think: what can I do? But sometimes we turn a blind eye to these things. My family comes from Vietnam and were very poor and it's important to have a better life.

An, university student, London. ■

In Focus, Summer 2005, Tourism Concern.

---

for us to see at first hand.

No longer faced with the anonymity and anomie which come with the territory of Western consumer culture, Sir and Madam find themselves bastions of privilege in a sea of poverty and deprivation. Fortunately, for our peace of mind, much of this translates into the picturesque or local color: kids on the beach flogging trinkets; women carrying jars of water on their heads; driving a hard bargain with local hawkers and knocking pennies off souvenirs. It's just like trade negotiations.

And for most of us it's so much easier to book a trip than to question the role of industrial consumer culture and the neoliberal agenda which makes our lives so unrelenting and our environments so devastated. No wonder we need to get away from it all.

4 Trouble in paradise

The idea of 'paradise' is central to much tourism promotion, with images of places and people designed to entice the tourist to spend money. However, the reality of 'paradise' is often poverty for the hosts.

FOR SOME, PARADISE is a stroll along an empty beach at sunset, while for others it might be a meal in a restaurant off the beaten track, or lounging beside a pool with a cold beer. For others, it may be wandering around ruins, or taking in a mountain vista.

One thing is generally certain about paradise, we believe we're more likely to experience it on holiday than at home. Going somewhere special and lovely is the whole idea of a holiday. But how does one person's poverty become another person's paradise?

The promise

To many of us a holiday offers a secular carrot of redemption, the nearest we can reasonably hope to get to a version of heaven. No wonder the promise of holiday happiness holds such sway in the collective imagination.

Philosopher Alain de Botton, for example, even sees a promise of paradise in a yellow plastic sign at Amsterdam's Schiphol Airport. Describing his 'delight' at the 'exotic' sign, he observes that 'if the sign provokes such pleasure, it is in part because it offers the first conclusive evidence of having arrived elsewhere. It is a symbol of abroad.'

He continues: 'Difference had to seem like an

The paradise paradox

The van people were talking about Goa and the good times you could have there, and my friend said to them, 'You mean people are starving in India and all you were doing was lying around on the beach?' ■

David Tomory, A Season in Heaven (Thorsons 1996).

improvement on what my own country was capable of [the sign suggested] vaguely, but intensely, that the country which had made it and which lay beyond... might in critical ways prove more congenial than my own to my temperament and concerns. The sign was a promise of happiness.'[1]

But rather than examine our own lifestyles and attitudes to discover the reasons for this apparent happiness deficit, we are encouraged to assign it a geographical and temporal location on earth: the holiday.

Consuming cultures

Although our individual concepts of paradise will vary, we tend to know when we've found it. All sorts of images are used by the travel industry to evoke different paradise products for the holidaymaker to consume: unpopulated palm-fringed beaches, swimming pools; tropical settings; attractive scenery; interesting food and markets; ancient monuments; wildlife; 'traditional' buildings and people – ideally smiling, clean, healthy and in 'ethnic' clothing.

All present an opportunity for the potential visitor to exercise consumer choice in the matter of surroundings, temperature, accommodation, things they might hope to see and do, experiences they might hope to have – dolphin-watching, getting drunk on cheap local alcohol, hurtling around on theme-park rides, gentle strolls absorbing the ambience, or lying on a beach fending off hawkers and skin cancer. The world, its people, environments and cultures are represented as a buffet of experiences from which the consumer can partake.

For many, beaches and sunshine have achieved cultural icon status, evoking a Pavlovian response of longing and relaxation just at the thought. Like other cultural icons – Madonna, Beckham, Coca-Cola – they have been constructed by advertising and the media to epitomize the good life.

Our own lives may not be so good, and the impossible ideals of consumer culture can never be fulfilled by ordinary mortals, but we can buy Beckham-endorsed sunglasses, or Madonna's CD, or a bottle of flavored sugary water and believe that we are somehow more.

For the tourist, freshly offloaded from a cramped flight, the warm tropical air saturated with the scents of flowers and less pollution, sends signals as clear as de Botton's: we have now officially arrived in Paradise. It is easy to overlook that this connection has only been part of our mass popular culture for the last 40 years or so, and that for much of the Global South it has yet to occur.

Paradise constructed

Naturally we tend not to examine paradise too closely for evidence that would contradict the illusion. In the same way that revelations about Beckham's alleged marital infidelities, or stories about Coke draining groundwater from south Indian villages might potentially damage their respective brands, we struggle to preserve the integrity of our personal holiday paradise by ignoring or dismissing elements of the scenario that may dent the happiness.

So the holiday brochure will not show Bali, Sri Lanka or the Maldives as places of rural poverty lacking in infrastructure, more or less repressive regimes, and with limited healthcare facilities or schools. That would not fit in with the island paradise image presented by government tourist offices and the travel industry.

Bali is indeed an exquisite and scenic island, with a strong sense of cultural pride and community cohesion. But in the last 25 years, development for the resort town of Kuta has meant that dirt roads have been widened and tarmacked and are now clogged with traffic. Small shops have been replaced by shopping malls, and simple local restaurants compete with

Trouble in paradise

Bali's tourism

At first glance the Bali of 2006 looks like a classic case of the tourism model of development turning sour. The bomb blasts in the main resort area of Kuta Beach in 2002 and 2005 have had a drastic effect on tourist numbers, with many Western governments warning their nationals against traveling to Indonesia, and Australians in particular tending to switch to Fiji as their 'island paradise' of choice. The result is that hotels, guest houses and restaurants all seem empty; taxi drivers and street sellers desperately compete for custom. A once-proud indigenous culture reduced to the squalid pursuit of Western dollars?

But probe only a little deeper and Bali tells a rather different story. Many people work in the tourist industry when numbers are greatest in the high season but revert to more traditional activities such as subsistence farming at other times of the year. Their village remains their home, and growing food provides the family baseline, while any extra income from the tourist industry provides for the luxuries that subsistence farming rarely allows. The same might be said of the island as a whole. Tourist dollars may leak away from grotesque global intrusions like Hard Rock Café and McDonald's, but they have also contributed to widespread electrification and free schooling that have vastly improved the quality of life over the last 25 years.

The Balinese soul, moreover, still seems amazingly resilient in the face of global monoculture, rooted in the peculiar mélange of animism and Hinduism that has sustained the island's people for centuries. Bomb outrages notwithstanding, the Balinese seem to have a considerable knack for taking what they want from tourism while continuing on their own sweet way. It is a knack that all too few other cultures affected by mass tourism seem to possess. ∎
Chris Brazier

McDonalds, Starbucks and KFC, while sex tourism is clearly in evidence. But there is some evidence of benefits to local people (see box 'Bali's tourism').

Fake paradise

The paradise constructed by marketeers, travel pages, tourist boards, travel agents and tour operators for consumers is a one-dimensional version of a place.

In this propaganda war, potential visitors are presented with a skewed image by those selling the holiday dream. Elements which don't fit in with this shiny reinvention are omitted or obliterated. Many of us somehow fail to be interested enough in the people and places we think we're visiting to find out the truth behind the media gloss.

Dreams or propaganda?

In the fantasy of a holiday paradise, reality has no place. This intentional mythologizing of people, place and experience is key to the re-invention of countries

Shankar

Quietly spoken Shankar is just recovering from a snakebite, his face thinner and more drawn than normal beneath his baseball cap. His passion is bodybuilding which he does at the Harry Potter gym. Thoughtful and serious, he describes himself as a businessman. He sells small stone carvings and postcards to tourists near the carved bas relief Arjuna's Penance in Mamallapuram.

'Stone carving is easy but selling to tourists is very difficult. I know they get annoyed and I don't want to disturb them but we need the money so I need to push them.

When we do business with tourists some are very kind, some just shout "No! No!" or "Go away! I don't want to buy anything." We feel angry but we're just trying to do business so we have to control ourselves, and we have to apologize. Some tourists get very upset and emotional, yelling. It's a bit stressful but we have to adjust.

Selling to tourists is very unpredictable, two days good, three days bad. I don't really like it but if I did nice work I'd only get Rp30-50/$1 a day. I'm the oldest son and my father only earns Rp1,900/$40 a month and my brother died, so I need to take care of my whole family. This is better paid, especially when you're a kid. Doing this I can earn Rp3-4,000/$80 a month.

I'd like to do some other work, nice work, like driving or being a welder but there's nothing else. I'm just waiting for my sister to get married then maybe a tourist will take me to Europe and I can do dishwashing or any other job, like housecleaner.

If I had money I wouldn't do this work but we need to live and there's nothing else I can do. When I was working as a kid I missed a lot of school and didn't get my exams. I used to study hard but now I'm too old to study. I worry about that. I can't write English and regret that I didn't work at school. I feel like I sacrificed my future for my family.' ∎

and places which are marketed for tourism. As Peter
Burns puts it: hosts and guests create myths about
each other and these myths can frame the temporary
relationships that arise.[2]

By accepting this made-over version of reality, we
become complicit in exploiting a sanitized and distort-
ed version of real life. Accepting an attractive illusion
as fact does nothing to foster the much-vaunted global
understanding of people and cultures promoted by the
travel trade as what tourism is all about. But when the
consumer's pleasure has primacy above all other values,
propaganda serves a vital purpose in enabling behavior
which might otherwise be questioned more rigorously.

So as tourist consumers we tend not to notice the
downside of our break. We see the impact of our
holiday as beneficial – providing jobs, perhaps some
cultural cross-pollination. We give them football
shirts and a taste for Western music; they sell us souvenirs and a feeling that a slower life is possible. Any
negative impacts like 'over-development', pollution,
or too many other tourists are seen as a process in
which we have little or no input. And if we are forced
to experience the reality of the rich world/poor world
gap, by being approached by beggars, hawkers or shop
workers, we may find this 'annoying'.

But for most the connection between our wealth
and their poverty will remain just one of those things:
a sad reflection of the way of the world and not something for which we have any personal responsibility.

In the sanitized 'holiday' reality, poverty, deprivation and disadvantage are photoshopped away. People
living on the streets because they have nowhere else
to go, or eking a fragile existence as a waiter, guide
or souvenir seller don't really compute with the exotic
glamour or unspoiled grandeur thing. That's why so
many of the holiday images are strangely empty, unoccupied territories for the tourist to claim as their own
personal piece of paradise.

Among some consumers from rich countries there has been a slow dawning of consciousness that their high standard of living comes at the expense of someone else's poverty and lack. But the majority still buy into the economic doctrine that price is king.

Knowing that global markets are loaded against the producers of say, coffee, and that workers in sweatshops are being exploited, does not necessarily translate into actions that may challenge the status quo. Understanding that the same is happening across the planet in the name of global tourism and holidays runs counter to decades of travel and consumer propaganda, not to mention our own desire to have a good time.

But at the end of the day, surely people are better off working in the comparatively clean and easy work of tourism, rather than the paddy fields?

The paddy fields question

Proponents of globalization and landless peasants converging on cities throughout the Majority World appear to have formed a coalition of intent. Just about anything is preferable to working on the land – hard, hot drudgery for a pittance.

Yet of course for much of human existence most people have worked on the land, producing something that even the hippest individual finds useful: food.

That this most fundamental of human activities has been downgraded, taken over by global agribusiness, and devastated by rich-world subsidies so as to become the last option for those with most experience doing it, is an indictment of the new economic order straddling the world.

So poor people are lured, like the tourists, into a seemingly better world. But we in the industrialized countries could create another version of tourism, one which at the very least provided a living wage and regular income, training and social provisions for the workers.

Trouble in paradise

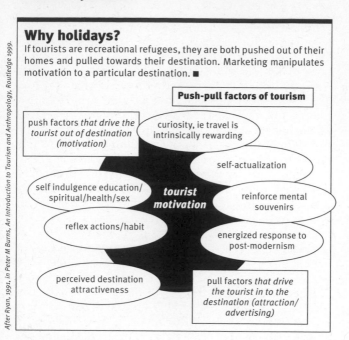

Why holidays?

If tourists are recreational refugees, they are both pushed out of their homes and pulled towards their destination. Marketing manipulates motivation to a particular destination. ■

Push-pull factors of tourism

push factors *that drive the tourist out of destination (motivation)*

curiosity, ie travel is intrinsically rewarding

self-actualization

self indulgence education/ spiritual/health/sex

reinforce mental souvenirs

tourist motivation

reflex actions/habit

energized response to post-modernism

perceived destination attractiveness

pull factors *that drive the tourist in to the destination (attraction/ advertising)*

After Ryan, 1991, in Peter M Burns, An Introduction to Tourism and Anthropology, Routledge 1999.

Parasitic tourism

When most tourists think about their impact on the host country and people, the consensus is that tourism is a good thing because it brings business and therefore money into the economy/country, to people who would otherwise be slaving away at something else less well-paid.

In this interpretation, tourism is a symbiotic process which benefits both host country and tourists. But it is becoming increasingly apparent that the relationship is more skewed as economic disparities underscore cultural prejudice and assumptions.

Paradise found?

In order to experience our holiday paradise, we need to understand what to expect. A palm-fringed beach could be many things: desolate, arid, hot and sweaty, wind-blown or just plain boring. It could be lonely, alienating, disturbing. We have been told so many times that such a beach equals pleasure that for many it has become the truth. Other images contribute to 'paradise' (see box, 'The tyranny of the image').

No natives

As seen in the box about brochures, local people are virtually excluded in the selling of paradise. The lack of interaction with people from the host country – apart from those in roles which tend to be subordinate – is confirmed by a tour operator who takes small groups to Latin America: 'The people on the tours just don't want to talk to the locals. It always surprises me. They've come all this way to see the country and experience the culture but at the end of the day they just all want to sit around and drink beer and talk to each other.'

The tyranny of the image

Graham Dann studied over 5,000 images featured on almost 1,500 pages of 11 British holiday brochures. He analyzed the language, and images used, deconstructing the 'consumerist myth' contained in them and was able to establish four types of paradise to be placed before the consuming public of potential tourists:

• Paradise contrived: no people; natives [sic] as scenery; natives as cultural markers

• Paradise confined: tourists only; tourist ghettos

• Paradise controlled: limited contact with locals; natives as servants; natives as entertainers; natives as vendors

• Paradise confused: further contact with natives, attempt to enter locals-only zones; natives as seducers, natives as intermediaries, natives as familiar, natives as tourists, tourists as natives

Dann observed that 'less than 10 per cent of the images were of tourists and locals shown together, an indication that, for the media-makers at least, the idea of tourism as a meeting of peoples was somehow not to be encouraged'. ∎

Peter M Burns, *An Introduction to Tourism and Anthropology* (Routledge 1999).

'Friendly natives'

A range of cross-cultural interactions becomes of heightened significance when there is a disparity between the visitor and the visited... the special rules that apply to willing hosts receiving invited guests into their homes are suspended [when] the transaction becomes a commercial one.' Problems arise when expectations have been raised:

• on the side of the 'host' where government campaigns have stressed or overstated the direct economic benefits arising from tourism

• on the part of the 'guest' who may have been exposed to exaggerated advertising literature from tour operators promoting the 'friendliness of the natives'. ■

Peter M Burns, *An Introduction to Tourism and Anthropology* (Routledge 1999).

A glance around any holiday venue from Malta to Marrakech will tell the same story. Tourists, even if not corralled into their own enclaves, will generally hang out with other tourists preferably from their own country. Because we don't speak the language, we don't really talk to local people except to order food or ask directions. And if we don't talk, how can we discover what their lives are like?

As Peter Burns notes: the commercial brochure can [be seen as] either a sop to existing fears and prejudices of potential tourists, or... as a deliberate construct setting out the rules of play before you go.

In either case it is a far cry from the explicit message of 'enjoying local culture' to be found in the same brochures: thus the brochure becomes, as Selwyn puts it, "an instrument not for greater democracy but for greater social and political control".[2]

Commercial tourism is part of the hospitality industry. We may be guests in a hotel or a guesthouse. We may be guests in a country. We may be visitors, or uninvited guests. We may be wanted or unwanted.

But the relationship is unequal because we have so much more economic power. Adopting the new religion of consumerism has taken away from many people the ability to think in any meaningful way about the impact of their lifestyle.

Industrial consumer culture imbues in its members a missionary zeal to convert non-believers (or non-consumers) into believers (consumers). This is seen as enabling them to have the economic benefits that we enjoy.

Building more factories, destroying species, eco-systems and cultures, and displacing populations in the global south is presented as normal and indeed the price of progress. Progress is achieved through rampant and infinite growth rather than a more sustainable lifestyle that is the solution to global inequalities.

Them and us

Imagine that your town is suddenly flooded with groups of African, Asian and Chinese tourists, all conspicuously wealthy. Coachloads appear in your local high street and start photographing you, your family and friends as you go about your daily business. The visitors never ask permission, as they speak no English, but it is clear that they consider the locals – you – exotic and strange.

Not only are the visitors dressed differently, and in a way which you find at best strange and at worst vulgar and disrespectful, but they demand their own kind of food, drinks and snacks. Despite being wealthy and staying in 5-star hotels, they attempt to bargain with cabbies, shopkeepers and anyone else they deal with.

You, your family and town are completely dependent on the goodwill and generosity of these strangers to make a living.

You see their leisured lifestyle, their extraordinary wealth; you and your friends are ordered around, patronized and occasionally yelled at by these super-rich strangers on whom you depend for a living.

And although the visitors find you, the way you organize and live your life and your home quaint, you understand very clearly that they believe that their way of life is infinitely superior to yours and that they are somehow better than you.

Would you feel happy and proud that they were coming to see your home? Grateful that you were able to earn a pittance by catering to their needs? Would you be offended by their behavior and styles of dress that you considered unsuitable? Would you think it was unfair that with all that money they haggled and bargained to get the lowest price? ■

The smiling imperative
Rowan is a New Zealander who has just traveled from Nepal to India. Speaking in a beach café within sight of ancient temples, she observes, 'In Nepal everyone is so friendly and welcoming.' She frowns. 'Here they're not like that. They really don't smile much at all.' ■

Those happy people

When Western tourists visit another country, particularly in the Majority World, they frequently say how 'happy' the locals are, commenting that they're 'always smiling, even if they don't have any money, they're happy'. And maybe they're happy because they're poor – and how reassuring is that?

But there can be many reasons for smiling. In Java it is considered bad manners not to smile when delivering bad news, the idea being that one doesn't want to further distress the recipient of the bad news by looking miserable.

What tourists may fail to realize is that, like other workers in the sales and hospitality industry, from receptionists, to PRs, to airline cabin crew, smiling is part of the job description. And those friendly hellos are often just a precursor to a sales pitch. Moving from a touristed area to a non-touristed area, say 20 km away, these hellos and attention will evaporate.

The quest for authenticity

Part of the tourist experience is the search for some kind of authentic aspect of life or culture in the host country. Places frequented by 'the locals' gain cultural cred, as do those deemed 'unspoilt'. Paradoxically, what often 'spoils' places is the presence of other tourists and the development of facilities – roads, car parks, cafés – which cater to the tourists' desire to experience that which was previously unspoilt. Similarly, the tourist culture may impinge on the local culture, for example with people wearing jeans

Dealing with tourists

Vishalaachi is selling moonstone trinkets and necklaces at a World Heritage Site in South India with her daughter, Uma.

'My husband has two wives and there's not enough money for us both. We need to eat. I have four children and I worry about them. My husband is a rickshaw driver. If he earns Rp200/$5 in one day, he pays Rp100/$2.50 to the owner, which leaves Rp100/$2.50 for six of us. What can you do with that? It's simply not enough to buy food, clothes, and everything else.

'There's no other work I can do. I'm not educated so I can't work in a shop, let alone a software company! If I do domestic work like washing up, I'd only earn Rp500/$12 a month, or Rp1,500/$36 if I worked for a company, but doing this I can earn Rp4,500/$100 a month if I'm lucky.

'I don't really like doing this work. If I had money I wouldn't do it. Why would I want to speak to strangers? I feel shy but I need to take care of my kids. Sometimes people say bad things about me because I'm a woman, especially if my husband isn't around.

'Foreigners can wear what they want to, but we just wear saris. We don't like seeing small clothes and bras. It's not our culture and it's not respectful. They may be poor in their own country, but here they're rich. Sometimes I feel, why weren't we born there. But their culture is bad. They're not clean, they do sex a lot. Sometimes they speak roughly to us, which is difficult.

'But I'm not involved with them, so I don't know their character. I just do my work and go home and forget about them. If I was rich I wouldn't bother talking nicely to them. It's just a living for me. I have my own life and concerns.'

'Small clothes'

Kumar owns a small bookshop in the tourist town of Mamallapuram in South India. A graduate and father of two daughters, he has been working with and observing tourists for over a decade.

'Nowadays Europeans are very well dressed, in churidars, saris. Before, many like small clothes... too much exciting! But still some people are very fresh and think it's the same as Europe – not full cover, shorts, sometimes walking along the road in a swimming costume. People laugh at them and make rude comments. I can understand why people do this. It's not the tourists' mistake, they want to wear what they want, it's a tropical country so they wear less dress. ∎

instead of more traditional dress.

Many tourists act as if their presence has no impact on the cultural life of the host country. But, particularly in heavily visited areas, exposure to lifestyles, attitudes and spending patterns which are often at odds with the host country's cultural norms can have an enormous effect on the local community.

According to anthropologist Bryan Turner, 'Tourism tends to make cultures into museums, as cultural phenomena which can be viewed as quaint, peculiar and local. Tourism, paradoxically, is a quest for authentic local cultures, but the tourist industry, by creating the illusion of authenticity... reinforces the experience of social and cultural simulation. The very existence of tourism rules out the possibility of authentic cultural experience.'[2]

Cultural brokers

When culture has become a commodity, interpreters – guides – are needed who can explain it to the visitor. These cultural brokers or 'marginal men' are the frontline soldiers in the battle for hearts, minds and foreign exchange between tourists and visitors.

With their exposure to different cultural norms, the guides absorb alternative cultural values as if by osmosis, becoming unwitting agents of cultural change within their own communities. However, this process of acculturation (see box) tends to be a one-way road.

Raj, a guide

'Even some guides don't respect our culture properly, they just know a tiny bit, not the important things like the Mahabharata [a major Sanskrit epic of ancient India]. Maybe they don't know all the gods properly. I don't know everything but I know some of the old stories because I listened to my older relatives and I was interested in the culture. I watched religious dramas in the village and asked older people about the religion, gods and culture.' ■

Guides who have been working with tourists since childhood and have been exposed to different cultural influences may start to imitate the behaviors of the visitors, 'on the basis that possession of them will lead to the leisured, hedonistic lifestyle demonstrated by the tourists.'[2]

Such people can become the unconscious carriers of the consumer culture virus. Alcoholism, gambling and other destructive behaviors are often the response of having to mediate these cultural conundrums.

Tourists can become role models for an unrealistic lifestyle, appearing both wealthy and indolent. This can lead to the development among local people of a sense of inferiority which can trigger a process of imitation.

As Raj, 26, a recovering alcoholic who's been working with tourists for nearly two decades, observes: 'In one way we like Western culture, but in one way we don't like. When foreigners are 15 or 17 they leave their home and family but we stay with our blood relatives till we die.' But he admits that he likes some

Trouble in paradise

aspects of Western culture. 'I like the freedom, not to worry about the family, maybe get divorced, not have children. Sometimes that seems nice, sometimes not.'

Hosts, guests and other lies

So our impact is significant. Are we visitors, guests, colonizers or invaders? Are they natives, hosts, colonized or invaded? Words can be used to clarify or obscure, but using an inaccurate term does not change the real nature of a thing. As 'colonials', Western tourists receive glamorous luxury (see box 'The colonial imperative').

Tanzania is one of the world's 49 Least Developed Countries (LDCs) as designated by the UN. Criteria for LDC status include low income (below $900 per capita), 'human weakness' based on indicators of nutrition, health, education and adult literacy

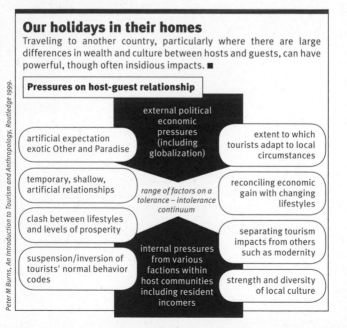

Peter M Burns, An Introduction to Tourism and Anthropology, Routledge 1999.

Our holidays in their homes

Traveling to another country, particularly where there are large differences in wealth and culture between hosts and guests, can have powerful, though often insidious impacts. ∎

Pressures on host-guest relationship

external political economic pressures (including globalization)

artificial expectation exotic Other and Paradise

extent to which tourists adapt to local circumstances

temporary, shallow, artificial relationships

range of factors on a tolerance – intolerance continuum

reconciling economic gain with changing lifestyles

clash between lifestyles and levels of prosperity

separating tourism impacts from others such as modernity

suspension/inversion of tourists' normal behavior codes

internal pressures from various factions within host communities including resident incomers

strength and diversity of local culture

The colonial imperative

Many travelers to East Africa are in search of not merely a life-changing encounter with the continent's wild animals, but also of an opportunity to be drawn into a reverie of grandeur and cosseting that bespeaks an earlier, more leisured era. 'Which is why we are the first to offer our clients the privileged opportunity to experience the newly created Grumeti Reserves in Tanzania's Serengeti,' says Dennis Pinto, New York-based Managing Director of Micato Safaris.

'Accommodation is designed to combine a colonial aura of service, luxury and wildlife with the comforts of home. Grumeti Reserves' secret of hospitality is its series of elegant lodgings and amenities expected by 21st century travelers, from plunge pools-with-a-view to the finest cuisine and wines. The sitting rooms and cottages of Saskawa Hill Lodge, with their grand piano, fireplaces, chintz, silver tea services and four poster beds, recall the Africa of Karen Blixen. Sabora Plains Tented Camp is a vision of khaki, beige, cream and fawn, where every amenity is provided in an atmosphere that recalls the romance of the 1930s. And Faru Faru River Lodge is a stunning combination of unspoiled nature and limitless luxury.' ■

Press release, ETN Travel News, New York 12 May 2006.

and generally unstable agriculture production and exports.[3]

The next chapter looks in more detail at this new form of colonialism.

1 Alain de Botton, *The Art of Travel* (Penguin Books 2003). 2 Peter M Burns, *An Introduction to Tourism and Anthropology* (Routledge 1999). 3 Jeremy Seabrook, *The No-Nonsense Guide to World Poverty* (New Internationalist/Verso 2003).

5 The new colonialism

Tourism has elements of colonialism in its global reach, relations with local inhabitants and impact on the global commons.

TAKING THEIR CUE from the tourism industry professionals, it is hardly surprising that most people see their holiday as an innocent way of relaxing. Alternative viewpoints take a less sanguine approach, highlighting the more problematic elements of this commercial transaction.

Realpolitik?

The view of tourism as a colonizing enterprise is echoed by Renato Soru, governor of the Mediterranean 'holiday' island of Sardinia, popular with the rich and famous such as Naomi Campbell, Silvio Berlusconi and Bill and Melinda Gates. In what has been seen by some as an assault on the upmarket tourist economy

---

Analyzing tourism

Modern tourism is a form of cultural imperialism, an unending pursuit of fun, sun and sex by the golden hordes of pleasure seekers who are damaging local cultures and polluting the world in their quest... tourism is an invasion outwards from the highly developed metropolitan centers into the 'uncivilized' peripheries. It destroys uncomprehendingly and unintentionally, since one cannot impute malice to millions of people or even to thousands of businessmen [sic] and entrepreneurs. ■

Turner, L and Ash, J, *The Golden Hordes*: International Tourism and the Pleasure Periphery (Constable 1975).

The modern tourist, 'like the trader, the employer, the conqueror, the governor, the educator or the missionary, is seen as the agent of contact between cultures and, directly or indirectly, the cause of change particularly in the less developed regions of the world.' ■

Nash, D *Current Anthropology*, 22 (5), 461-81 (1989) 'Tourism as a Form of Imperialism' in Peter M Burns, *An Introduction to Tourism and Anthropology* (Routledge 1999).

of the island, Mr Soru has slapped heavy harbor dues on all non-Sardinian boats, as well as putting a 20 per cent tax on the buying and selling of second homes within 3 km (1.9 miles) of the sea as part of a strategy to protect the coastline from further development. He has spoken of tourism industry as a form of pseudo-colonial exploitation, 'not much different from the 19th and early 20th centuries'.[1]

The average tourist, smeared with factor 28, sipping on a soft drink and enjoying the rhythmic sounds of the waves, might seem an unlikely, if not downright bizarre, candidate for the role of a new colonial.

People can no longer deny the global inequalities created by governments and TNCs, and all too often, perpetuated by consumer apathy. Whether it is supermarkets excluding small producers of lettuces; corporations forcing down wages for poor farmers; or high street stores producing cheap clothes using sweatshop labor, consumers are increasingly aware of their role in keeping the poor in poverty.

A holiday may appear to have nothing whatsoever in common with a lettuce, but the operating systems producing these are remarkably similar, and have similar outcomes (see 'The holiday as a lettuce' box page 88).

One difference between buying a supermarket lettuce and a holiday is that with a holiday we can experience global inequalities at first hand. We can see the discrepancy between our standards of living and those of the local inhabitants, particularly in the

The holiday as a lettuce: The Gambia

Britain and the Netherlands account for two-thirds of all international tourists [in the Gambia] and British tourists benefit from the purchasing power of the major UK operators who feature The Gambia. Large tour operators function... like supermarket chains – they contract in bulk on our behalf and secure good [cheap] prices which UK tourists are pleased to accept.

European consumers are the beneficiaries of the purchasing power of the large operators but, while low prices are good for tourists, they are not good for The Gambia. Concern in the country about the growth of all-inclusive holidays led to attempts by the government to ban them, but a storm of protest from European operators resulted in the policy being abandoned. The real issue is about how much of the tour operators' and tourists' expenditure remains in The Gambia. ∎

Harold Goodwin and Adama Bah, 'The Gambia: Paradise or Purgatory', *Developments* (DFID, Third Quarter 2004).

Majority World. Our impact is visible and immediate. We may be annoyed and upset by poor people trying to 'cheat us' (read: 'make a fragile living and redressing the global inequalities'). We can see and experience unspoilt beaches/scenery/traditional cultures before the industrialization which has largely destroyed them in the North does the same there.

As we recognize this, we can understand that we are using the South as a playground and resource, reinventing a colonial pattern of dominance. Wherever the concerned holidaymaker chooses to look, once eyes are open to the reality that travel and tourism are a new (or reinvented) form of colonialism, evidence is plentiful and disturbing. Whether it's the waiter dependent on tips, hotel staff on short-term contracts, or the coconut seller scratching a living on the fringes of the global tourism empire, workers get a raw deal.

A lot of the time such people are almost invisible to tourists, doing the backroom work – cooking, cleaning, driving and generally facilitating our pleasure. It's comforting to assume that 'they're better off working in tourism than in the paddy fields'. No-one wants to imagine that the people serving them are unhappy. Many holidaymakers would be appalled to realize the truth of the service staff's situations.

According to Tourism Concern, of the four major companies – First Choice, My Travel, Thomas Cook and TUI – which control over 50 per cent of mass tourism bookings out of the UK, in 2002 only First Choice had an employee working specifically on social responsibility.

Tourism Concern has researched the labor conditions in the tourism industry in their Sun, Sand, Sea and Sweatshops campaign. The reports they have compiled from across the world show that workers in the tourism industry suffer from exploitative labor

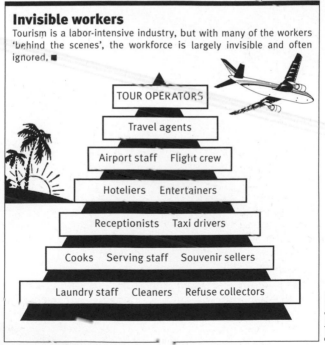

Invisible workers

Tourism is a labor-intensive industry, but with many of the workers 'behind the scenes', the workforce is largely invisible and often ignored. ■

TOUR OPERATORS

Travel agents

Airport staff   Flight crew

Hoteliers   Entertainers

Receptionists   Taxi drivers

Cooks   Serving staff   Souvenir sellers

Laundry staff   Cleaners   Refuse collectors

Tourism Concern

The new colonialism

conditions, over-dependency on tips, long working hours, unpaid overtime, stress, lack of secure contracts, little or no training and virtually no prospects of promotion (see box 'Hidden people').

Hearts and minds
But for some resort owners, staff not only have to smile; their souls and emotions are colonized. For example, workers in a new resort in the Seychelles

---

Hidden people
Mexico
In Mexican resorts such as Cancun, the cost of living is high and not matched by wages. Ninety per cent of hotel workers get only the minimum wage. Average salaries are rarely above $4 per day, while an apartment can cost $150 a month. Hotels often hire staff for 28 days then let the contract expire and recruit the worker again. Staff frequently work 12-14 hour days and commute for an hour to their lodgings. Many workers live in huts made of carton and wood with an outside toilet.

As a result of rural migration to hotspots like Cancun and the Maya Riviera, workers can suffer from social alienation, the disintegration of families and abuse of alcohol and drugs. Separated by geographical distance and with only six days' holiday a year, they are displaced from their own families and communities.

And even the beaches – famed for white, powdery sand and clear, turquoise water – are off limits. Although state-owned, apart from one, they have been de facto privatized to hotels and are accessible only by customers of the resorts.

Comments Araceli, an activist, 'The luxury of the hotels is not reflected at all by the living standards of the workers. All the incoming money is invested in further building enterprises and never reaches the workers.'

In the **Canary Islands**, waiter supervisor Santiago had to take six months off work due to depression. 'Many workers leave because of the pressure. Many have even had a whole year off. Now I'm managing with the help of anti-depressants. My boss is trying to make me give up the job. They even control the time I spend in the toilet.'

Carmen, a room-cleaner says, 'People in higher positions treat us like inferior human beings. Working as a room cleaner is very hard. I have to clean 23 rooms... or 26 if a workmate is off. My job is really hard, physically and emotionally, and many young people leave, but

must spend 20 minutes meditating to 'clear their minds of worldly worries' so they do not pass on stress to Western guests.

And before they're employed, many may have to pass an 'emotional quotient index' to check that they're emotionally balanced. The idea is to create a calm atmosphere at the £1,000/$1,875 a night Maia Resort. Managing Director Richard Wellers comments, 'We're going to get lots of executives staying

---

I have no choice. Some of the tourists see we are educated and have consideration towards us but others think that we are their slaves and don't treat us well. Going on holiday is a luxury I could never afford.'

The **Dominican Republic** is the most popular tourist resort in the Caribbean. With its clear seas and miles of sandy beaches, it boasts the largest all-inclusive resort industry in the world, with 50,000 rooms. But 90 per cent of the island's 8.6 million residents live below the poverty line despite the highest economic growth in the Americas from 1996-2000.

Consuela, a chambermaid, is attempting to bring up two teenage children on her own. 'Our salaries are not enough to satisfy our main necessities like food, clothes, housing, electricity and water. Every day we think about what we're going to eat and how we're going to pay for the electricity. We have to smile to the tourists but it is not what we are feeling in our souls. We want to work and we want to make your holidays happy. But it is difficult.'

Consuela is often paid several months in arrears and so has to take out loans to cover basic living costs, so that when her salary arrives it is quickly spent on paying off these debts, leaving the family penniless and wanting. She speaks for millions in the global tourism industry when she says, 'We don't have anyone to appeal to, laws do not exist, they do not cover us and if we complain it would be worse for our job.'

She would like to join a trade union but the hotel has not agreed to have one on the premises.

In four-star hotels in **Kenya** used by mainstream UK operators, one group of waiters said that they earned the equivalent of 20p/38c per hour and that if they receive tips they can then buy soap to wash with. A perk of the job is that they can wash at the hotels where they work. One hotel, Sun and Sand, has fountains playing at the entrance while immediately opposite in the village there is just one tap. ∎

Tourism Concern, *Sun Sea, Sand and Sweatshops* 2005
www.tourismconcern.org.uk

here. They have very stressful lives. They don't want to feel other people's stress when they get to us.'[2]

Perhaps providing a fair wage, decent living conditions, staff training, holidays and promotion prospects would do the trick equally as well, if not better.

Decent wages

Many holidaymakers think that workers are better off having a job in the tourism industry than doing agricultural or factory work, or being unemployed. This is then used as a justification for paying people less than the legal wage or insufficient to cover basic living expenses. 'The fact that in some parts of the world people are desperate for work is no justification for exploitation,' says Tourism Concern.

Compounding the argument for a living wage is that as long as poor people effectively pick up the tab for rich Western holidaymakers, they will remain in poverty. This translates into not being able to eat, not being able to have proper medical treatment, not being

---

Sun and sweatshops

Tour operators have a clear responsibility to ensure that their profits are not built on cost-cutting and abusive labor standards. They [need to ensure] that they are not colluding with their suppliers and making profits when the people who work in this supply chain are denied their basic human rights as laid out in international and national legislation. Other industries, such as the extractive and clothing industries have been checking or auditing their supply chains for many years. Tour operators are making some headway in their policy statements about their commitment to Corporate Social Responsibility (CSR), but these rarely include labor issues for destination countries.

Many multinational companies have signed up to international agreements, such as the UN Global Compact, which aim to protect workers' rights. However these agreements are not legally enforceable and tend to be sidelined when they conflict with other business pressures. The same applies to voluntary corporate codes of conduct which are frequently criticized for being public relations tools. ■

Tourism Concern, *Sun, Sand, Sea and Sweatshops*, 2005
www.tourismconcern.org.uk

---

able to send children to school. Why should poor people subsidize the holidays of the rich?

Tour operators sell an extraordinary profitable product, but they are making money from labor practices which take advantage of poor and vulnerable people, particularly in the Global South. If the T&T industry is as concerned about eradicating poverty as it asserts, why does it consistently fail to address these issues?

However, there are signs that the industry is being forced into a reluctant acknowledgement that exploitative business-as-usual practices are less and less acceptable. In a joint initiative with the Prince of Wales International Business Leaders Forum (IBLF), the UNWTO has announced the creation of the Tourism and Human Rights Initiative. However, whether yet another impressively named but voluntary initiative will make any real difference to the lives of people like Consuela remains to be seen.

According to Dawid de Villiers, special advisor to UNWTO on ethical matters: 'To be truly effective, the tourism industry needs to take a comprehensive approach to human rights, encompassing a wide spectrum of human rights issues, including but not limited to: concerns around child and bonded labor, workplace health and safety, commercial exploitation of children, the exploitation of migrant workers, discrimination and displacement of indigenous people and other vulnerable groups.'[3]

However, both this tick-box approach and the fact that it is presented in the context of a business case for corporate responsibility, suggest that this could be yet another case of T&T greenwash. It is noticeable that in all the talk of 'responding to challenges', 'specific sector dilemmas' and 'benchmarking performance' there is no mention of applying existing legislation to give workers a fair wage and decent conditions.

The demand-end of the holiday chain tends to be given far more consideration than the supply-end. This

93

could be construed as yet another version of colonial attitudes, except that this is a modern industry which is supposedly in favor of equal opportunities, human rights, peace creation and poverty alleviation.

As the industry acknowledges, more evidence of the uptake of CSR in the tourism industry is urgently required. According to Dr Graham Miller of the University of Surrey, England, 'the industry can only maintain a low profile for so long before changes heralded by the adoption of CSR in the corporate world will also be required in the tourism industry'. He adds that all tourism businesses should learn the lessons of other industries and document their environmental responsibilities now, before profits are threatened, customers and suppliers are lost and the survival of their business is compromised.

Economic power as exploitation

Sex tourism is at one end of an exploitative global continuum in which the needs of the least powerful are subsumed to those with more economic power. The argument about workers in the tourism industry that 'they're better off than their compatriots/working in the paddy fields' is used ad nauseam to justify unfair practices. It is popular among certain sectors of the holidaymaking public who are reluctant to acknowledge the part they play in exploiting their fellow humans in the tourism industry.

Sex tourism

Colonialist attitudes are particularly clear in the area of sex tourism. Whether this involves children or adults – many of whom will be women working in the sex industry because of abuse, coercion or lack of any other way to earn a living, tourism for sexual purposes highlights the new colonial attitude of some holidaymakers when they visit the Global South.

But there are plenty of people who see the sex

industry as offering a better life for the sex workers. (see box 'Harmless fun?').

The issues of sex tourism and child sex tourism are increasingly on the international agenda. ECPAT (End Child Prostitution in Asian Tourism) UK, which campaigns against child sex tourism, has worked with industry magazine Travel Weekly to raise awareness of the realities of child sex tourism. Their voluntary Code of Conduct for the Protection of Children from Sexual Exploitation in Travel and Tourism is being implemented by more than 45 companies worldwide. Only three UK companies are participating: TUI UK, First Choice and The Gambia Experience.

Throbbing sex

'Sex industry throbs with tourism boom,' blared the headline of a Philippines-based publication Manila Standard Today, highlighting the spots and various ways that prostitution is flourishing with foreign tourists in the country. The report depicts growing concern as Southeast Asia emerges to be one of the world's top destinations for people seeking sex with children.

The new colonialism

'The tourism program of the government which aims to project the Philippines as a major tourist destination has increased the number of prostituted women,' says Gabriela, a women's group. 'As more and more areas of the country are targeted for tourism, more and more women are driven to prostitution in desperation to ensure their family's survival.'

The Department of Tourism (DoT) has denied any link between prostitution and tourism. Assistant secretary for tourism planning and promotion at DoT, Eduardo Jarque Jr, comments, 'Other countries have the same problem. We just can't control it. Foreigners find us very friendly. [Their] enjoyment here is very high.'

Employment in hotels and restaurants has grown in the last year from 836,000 to 866,000.[4]

Uncomfortable linkages can be drawn between the exploitation of child and adult sex workers in the Global South and the tourism industry. So long as industrialized countries have the whip hand, economically speaking, over the Majority World, the complicity of the average Northern consumer – whether of MP3 players, sugar or holidays – is a key factor in keeping the majority of the world's population poor. And time and again, in many parts of the world, increased tourism means more sexual

---

Harmless fun?

Bar girls and masseuses in Bangkok can earn Baht 20,000-50,000 ($535-$1,400) per month, which is more than ten times the average per capita income in Thailand. It is therefore a debatable question whether the girls are the prey or predators in this game, but either way there is no question that they are economically much better off and far more independent than the overwhelming majority of their compatriots. Regardless of what high-minded farangs [foreigners] may think, most of these girls consider themselves lucky to be working in glamorous, air-conditioned Bangkok, doing what basically falls into the categories of sanuk [fun] and sabai [feeling good]. If you feel guilty about the low cost of sex in Bangkok, don't abstain – instead give more and help put a Thai brother through college! ■

Lee Daniel, *Bangkok by Night* (MPC 1988).

exploitation of women and children.

Thai Professor Prawase Wasi notes links between hedonism, consumerism and exploitation: 'It cannot be denied that the tourism boom [in Thailand] is linked to the escalation in prostitution.' He continues that 'prostitution is an integrated social pathology and the prevalence of child prostitution lays bare fundamental attitudes inherent in Western society, the rotten moral core of a worldview based on affluence as the primary criteria. This way of thinking has spread to other parts of the world.' And he concludes that while exchange visits between people of different nationalities are desirable and should be encouraged, 'Tourism is no longer exchange visits, it is a one-way business, the rich benefiting from the poor and the poor trying to extract from the rich.' And this brings us on to the question of human rights.

Human rights

When discussing human rights, there can be a slipperiness: whose rights do we mean? One person or group's rights may be in opposition to another's. It depends who you're talking to and who you're talking about. Someone from a rich nation might assume it is their right to work hard and have a cheap holiday,

---

All that Glitters

Former glam rock star Gary Glitter has been arrested in Vietnam where police want to question him about alleged child sex offences. The 61-year-old was detained at Ho Chi Minh airport as he tried to board a plane to Bangkok. An immigration official recognised his name from a newspaper article, state-controlled media reported.

A newspaper reported that police were investigating Glitter over allegations of 'obscene acts with a child'.

Glitter was expelled from Cambodia in 2002, although no specific reason was given for his deportation. He was convicted in the UK in 1999 of possessing child pornography and served two months in jail. ■

BBC 19 November 2005 www.bbc.co.uk

---

whilst at the same time denying their waiter the right to decent living conditions. What happens when the tourist's right to a dip in the pool with a relaxing shower afterwards clashes with the local people's rights to drinking water?

The kind of double standard seen in the box ('Tourists 24') is ever present in the world and remarkably little analyzed or challenged by tourists. Take the impact of recreational activities such as golf.

Hole in one

It seems unlikely at first thought that a round of golf could cause anyone anywhere any problem. But a Tourism Concern report by Anita Pleaumarom, called 'Golf and Tourism', focused on the explosion of golf courses in Thailand and provides some insights. Catering to the affluent, particularly the Japanese, 'New golf projects, usually in the style of country clubs, luxurious hotels and residential complexes, have been mushrooming in almost all parts of the country. It [is] assumed that many of these projects are owned by foreigners...'

Golf courses all over the world leave permanent scars on the landscape, with natural vegetation destroyed and huge amounts of soil removed to shape the greens and to create artificial lakes. Plant and animal habitats are destroyed, as the fairways and greens have no ecological value at all. Even though the grass may look fresh and green it bears hardly any life.

Tourism Concern notes that: 'Wasting a huge amount of water on golf courses interferes with the water flow in surrounding areas, drying up ponds, marshes, spring waters and underground water, causing land subsidence. This causes a lack of drinking water and water for irrigation for local farmers.'

The report adds that turning farmers into caddies seems to be 'perfectly in line with the national development policy to change agricultural Thailand into a Newly Industrialized Country (NIC), and the seventh National Economic and Social Development Plan which aims at reducing the numbers of farmers to a mere 17 per cent within the next five years'.

Cruised off

Another growing activity is cruise ship holidays. Cruise ships are good case studies in how to cause environmental damage and pollution. They are a key part of the global T&T industry, and run by conglomerates such as the Disney Corporation.

A typical cruiser will carry around 2,000 passengers with 900 crew. In the wake of 9/11, bookings have increased with 11 million passengers every year. A big increase has been in North Americans to the Caribbean.

In a familiar pattern, labor standards, pay and

Tourists: 24, local people: 0
Residents of Sinqerim village in Goa were refused their request for piped water for one or two hours a day and now have to rely on well water. The nearby Taj Holiday Village and Fort Aguada complex have a constant 24 hour supply of water which is piped underneath the village. ■

Tourism Concern www.tourismconcern.org.uk

conditions are generally extremely low, with workers from Majority World countries servicing the wealthy travelers for a pittance.

Ross Klein of Cruisejunkie.com asserts that 'Cruises' impact on the natural environment can no longer be ignored. They have repeatedly resisted conversion to low sulfur fuels despite the environmental advantages. They contribute to air pollution when using incinerators in or near port areas, and affect marine ecosystems with toxic discharges and anchorage. Sewage is discharged at sea. They operate with little regulation, virtually no monitoring and voluntarily decide whether or not to respect island coastal waters.'[5]

The UNWTO apparently has few worries about climate change (see box). People may be frying and collapsing from heat stroke, there may be hurricanes,

---

'Climate change poses risk to tourism, UNWTO warns'

Climate change poses a growing risk to the tourism industry, the tourists themselves and economies that rely on their spending,' UNWTO chief Francesco Frangialli has said. But to combat this, 'more research is needed and closer co-ordination between governments and the tourism sector to ensure that possible effects are factored into tourism policies and development and management.'

According to the UNWTO, beach destinations, winter sports resorts and outdoor activities are all highly dependent on favorable climate conditions. But extreme weather conditions, such as hurricanes and floods, threaten the health and safety of tourists and host populations alike and can destroy the infrastructure of a destination... These images can dissuade potential tourists from traveling, with the consequent downturn in tourist numbers hitting the local economy.

Climate change can also transform the natural environment that attracts tourists in the first place – eroding coastlines, damaging coral reefs and other sensitive eco-systems, or limiting snowfall in mountainous regions as well as affecting basic services like water supplies, especially during periods of peak demand.

However, it's not all bad news: the alterations in weather patterns could provide new opportunities for the tourism industry, particularly by increasing the number of visits in previously off-peak months. ■

UNWTO media release in TravelPress.biz, 7 November 2005.

floods and extreme weather, but the industry's revenues will continue to be boosted.

New kind of refugee

Climate change is also likely to impact in other ways, including people seeking refuge from its outcomes. The UN has warned that by 2010 as many as 50 million people will be fleeing from the effects of environmental destruction, including 'slow moving catastrophes' like desertification, diminishing safe water supplies and climate change-induced sea level rise. Unlike victims of political violence or 'natural disasters' like the Southeast Asian Tsunami, the Pakistan earthquake or hurricane Katrina, 'environmental refugees' are not recognized under international law and do not benefit from millions of dollars' support from public and private funds.

The director of the UN University for Environment and Human Security, Janos Bogardi, has said that environmental refugees may have to be considered as a 'new category of refugee'.[6]

The European Union's justice commissioner, Rocco Buttiglione, has commented that European asylum rules are unclear about how to deal with immigrants whose environment has been destroyed by natural catastrophes, such as drought or famine in Africa.

Not joined up

This lack of joined-up thinking around the connection between tourism, air travel, greenhouse gases and climate change is highlighted by a paper presented by Geoffrey Lipman, special advisor to the UNWTO's Secretary-General, at a meeting of World Economic Forum (WEF) Governors at Davos in 2004. The WEF is an exclusive invitation-only gathering of leaders of business, government, international organizations and the media. Assembled plutocrats were treated to a paper on Tourism, aviation and poverty reduction. This document produced a number of assertions, suggesting that 'in the world's poorest countries, with the right policies, tourism can be a major export and primary development tool. Its key point is that competitively priced, frequent air service is a core component of tourism and in turn a major tool for poverty reduction'.

'The wealth created spreads rapidly across domestic economies', it continues, 'wherever tourist facilities are established and local suppliers plugged in – including in poor rural areas... It's a huge job creator with good opportunities for women and young people.' Case studies, figures or any other kind of evidence are not presented.

Presumably an added benefit for the poor of becoming 'part of the exporter chain' (see box, 'Taking Wing') is that they can then compete on an equal footing with multi-billion dollar TNCs.

Others express a different point of view on the impact of climate change on the world's poor. According to Archbishop Desmond Tutu, 'the world's wealthiest countries have emitted more than their fair share of greenhouse gases. Resultant floods, droughts and other climate change impacts continue to fall disproportionately on the world's poorest people and countries, many of which are in Africa. Africa and climate change are intrinsically linked. The richest countries in the world... have a responsibility to help the poorest. This is not charity but a moral obligation.'[7]

Flight data
We know that flying is a major contributor to climate

Turning up the heat
In France in 2003, an 'unprecedented' heatwave caused the deaths of around 15,000 people. August 2003 was the hottest summer on record in Europe, and researchers attributed it directly to climate change. ■

'Millions to flee climate disasters by 2010, UN warns', www.via3.net, 17 October 2005.

chaos, although there is no reference by the UNWTO to this. And the average holidaymaker doesn't want to think about it either. As reported by Amanda Brown, PA environment correspondent in The Scotsman: 'According to the UK Government, greenhouse gases from aircraft rose by almost 90 per cent between 1990 and 2003. The boom in low-cost air travel is partly blamed for the huge rise. Over the same period, CO_2 emissions from industry dropped by 21 per cent and those from domestic users by 3 per cent. Transport emissions (excluding international aviation and shipping) were up 8 per cent, although the rate of increase has slowed in recent years.

UK Environment Minister Elliot Morley said that the rise in greenhouse gases from aviation fuel 'is partly due to the cost of air travel falling across the board and the impact of low-cost airlines'.[8]

But, conveniently for the international T&T industry, aviation emissions are not included in the Kyoto Agreement. If they were, 'the UK's total greenhouse gas emissions would be about 5 per cent greater.' In addition, the airline industry enjoys substantial tax breaks on aviation fuel.

The UK Government has estimated the environmental costs alone of air transport per flight. This ranges from £245/$465 for a B 737-400, to £2,499/$4,700 for a B 767-300, to a massive £5,140/$9,750 for a B 747-400. This is the amount by which the British tax-payer is effectively subsidizing the aviation fuel costs of the airline industry.

Carbon lies

But what about the newest industry that is emerging to soothe our consciences – carbon offsetting? This process of working out the amount of CO_2 we generate on a flight and then offsetting it by paying an organization to plant a tree, is touted by many (including concerned popstars, so it must be OK) as the have-it-all solution to flying around the planet. The only problem is, carbon offsetting doesn't work. It merely slows down climate change: the only way to reduce emissions is not to create them. And by providing a false sense of business as usual, it reinforces the notion that we can still hop on a plane as and when we so desire, and buy our way out of the consequences.

In the same way that sponsoring a child used to be seen as an acceptable way of helping relieve poverty, sponsoring a tree to offset climate change encourages

---

The price of 'progress'?

China is the world's second biggest producer of greenhouse gas emissions and is expected to overtake the United States as the biggest, bringing acid rain to roughly a third of the country and poisoning nearly three quarters of rivers and lakes.

People all over the country have rioted and held demonstrations over pollution damaging their crops in the countryside and affecting children's health. Smog is a much bigger issue among Chinese people than democracy, internet freedom, censorship or the right to worship. Breathing comes first.

The World Bank, which says that 16 of the world's 20 most polluted cities are in China, estimates that 400,000 people here die a year from air pollution-related illnesses. ∎

'Doctors tell you not to go outside', *The Independent* 13 June 2006.

Flying: just say no!

'Seductive voices are telling us that we can continue to fly as much as we do and not harm the environment by using carbon offsets. Those arguments just do not stand up. All they do is shield us from the harsh reality. The 'jump-in-a-plane-for-a-weekend-break' culture that has grown up in the rich world is doing environmental and social harm. We need to ditch carbon offsets and face up to that harsh reality.' ∎

John Stewart, Heathrow Airport Campaign Against Noise/Clear Skies in CO2NNED! *New Internationalist* 391, July 2006.

the rich world consumer to carry on enjoying the fruits of global inequality while the poor continue to pay for our pleasure with their health, wellbeing and lives.

We need to kick the fossil-fuel habit and take responsibility for our emissions. Investing in renewables and socially and environmentally responsible tree-planting is not a license to pollute. As Soumitra Ghosh of the National Forum of Forest Peoples and Forest Workers in India put it: 'We're creating a sort of 'climate apartheid' wherein the poorest and darkest-skinned pay the highest price – with their health, land, and in some cases, their lives – for the continued carbon profligacy of the rich'.[9]

1 'Sardinia targets yachts in battle against rich tourists', *The Independent*, 3 June 2006. **2** 'Waiter, you're stressing me out', *The Times*, 27 May 2006. **3** 'UNWTO and IRLF Announce a New Human Rights Initiative for The Tourism Industry', eTN Press, 17 March 2006. **4** 'Sex industry throbs with tourism boom', eTN, 30 March 2006. **5** 'Cruise Industry: Sailing in Troubled Waters', 27 March 2006, eTurbonews.com **6** 'Millions to flee climate disasters by 2010, UN warns', www.via3.net, 17.10.2005. **7** 'Stop Climate Chaos... or Africa gets it', www.wwf.org.uk/onlinecampaigner **8** 'Cheap Flights Blamed for Aircraft Greenhouse Gas Rise', *The Scotsman* 30 June 2005. **9** Soumitra Ghosh, National Forum of Forest Peoples and Forest Workers in CO2NNED!, *New Internationalist* 391, July 2006.

6 Tourism as politics

From the push for economic 'development' at the cost of the environment, livelihoods and cultures, to the annexation of ancestral lands for the creation of wildlife reserves and eco-tourism, tourism is a political activity.

IN THE RUSH to open up more and more areas for tourism, rarely is a dissenting voice heard questioning the desirability of this form of luxury consumerism. Government ministers and business people love tourism and there is a general assumption that it is not only desirable, but that it performs a vital function in generating income and attracting foreign exchange. As we have seen, for local people it is often a different, and less happy story.

Even former UN Secretary-General Kofi Annan believes in its apparently redemptive power. Addressing the UNWTO summit in April 2006, he asserted: 'Tourism really has the potential of opening up economic space for people round the world. We should encourage developers to go and set up tourist developments,' and in doing so help provide basic amenities and 'uplift' the local people, 'encouraging them to produce for the tourists.'

Hearts and minds

As well as having a voice in the UN as a specialized agency (UNWTO), the global tourism industry conducts an ongoing PR presence to convince people of its altruistic intentions. The extent to which it has succeeded is spectacular. Francesco Frangialli, UNWTO secretary-general, puts it like this: 'Tourism has the capacity to contribute decisively to the fight against poverty'. As always, the mechanisms by which this is supposed to happen are conspicuous by their absence. Away from the rhetoric, quieter, less well-known voices struggle to be heard.

People in the Majority World have been aware of this for some time. In 1991, tourism activist and researcher Sudarat Srisang noted that 'Tourism favored by governments like Thailand does not solve the problems of national economics and mass poverty. On the contrary, it rather increases the dependency on multinational companies and the integration into the global capitalist economy. It is mainly the ruling class which benefits from this form of tourism.'[1]

As KT Suresh from Equations in India observes: 'The development of a sector is not solely dependent on factors within the sector. It is influenced by the general socio-economic environment, the political system and the policy framework... Tourism Policy would not have evolved on its own without being influenced by the general tenor of macro-economic policy. Tourism policy thus has a socio-political grounding as much as a macro-economic coloring.[2]

In a detailed analysis of the way in which the structural adjustment program initiated in 1992 impacted on tourism, Suresh quotes from the then government's

Tourism as politics

Annual Plan: 'The future growth of tourism will have to be through private initiatives. The State will contribute to tourism by planning broad strategy of development, provision of monetary and fiscal initiatives to catalyze private sector investment.'

This pattern is common in Majority World countries opening up their tourism sector. Suresh notes that 'environmental considerations were thrown to the winds and there were large-scale human rights violations... privatization meant the alienation of the majority of our population and their deprivation.'

This scenario is at the root of much, if not all, tourism development, particularly in the Majority World, and is one of the reasons why the current neo-liberal model of tourism is both problematic and harmful. It is, all too often, the reality behind the T&T industry's political spin of so-called poverty alleviation.

It's not just activists who challenge the theories of economic trickle-down. The World Bank's 2003 Extractive Industries Review report 'Striking a Better Balance' found that 'increased investments have not necessarily helped the poor; in fact, oftentimes the environment and the poor have been further threatened

Big Tourism

Tourism is a major earner, and the poorer the country, the larger the percentage of earnings from the sector. In 2005, WTTC predicted that the industry would contribute almost 11 per cent of global GDP and create 220 million jobs. ■

Tourism earnings as a share of all services (%) 2000	
OECD countries	28.1
European Union	28.5
Developing countries	43.3
Least developed countries (LDCs)	70.6

UN World Tourism Organization

by the expansion of a country's extractive industries sector... the World Bank Group does not appear to be set up to effectively facilitate and promote poverty alleviation through sustainable development in extractive industries in countries it assists.'[3]

Why governments love tourism

Suresh makes a key point about governments' fondness for tourism when he observes: 'This smokeless industry has the advantage of generating maximum value-added, because of low-cost inputs.'[2]

This rarely articulated point is worth examining. Unlike, say, the more commonly thought-of extractive industries, such as mining or petrochemicals, tourism is perceived by many (including politicians) as a quick and easy means of generating substantial income and providing employment simply by utilizing something – beaches, attractive landscape, local customs and people – that is already there. The impact of tourism on these 'natural resources' is rarely considered, although occasionally the concept of 'sustainable' is used, generally more as a marketing tool rather than signaling that the impact of tourism on land, livelihoods and communities will be seriously addressed.

Industrial tourism

An analysis of the implications of tourism as a trade export item in Third World economies by Tourism Concern demonstrated that 'far from bringing economic benefits, tourism to the South tended to exacerbate poverty, inequality and socio-cultural and environmental degradation. Globalization and trade liberalization have tended to undermine small-scale local producers and economies... In many developing countries the cost of introducing tourism as an industry can be higher than the benefits, particularly for disadvantaged local communities.'

While the *spinmeisters* of the tourism industry

Mohan

A guide in his late twenties, Mohan has been working with tourists for nearly two decades in Mamallapuram, Tamil Nadu, India. Fiercely proud of his Tamil culture and heritage and a devout Hindu, he has taught himself English, French, German, Japanese and Hindi.

'When I was eight I sold postcards to tourists. I started with one postcard, then two, then a set. It was an income. In one way I liked it. I'd use the money as pocket money to buy pens, schoolbooks, food for my family, anything. But in another way I felt it was like begging. I'm a pure Indian and I know what the English people [the British Raj] did to us and that we were like servants. Working with tourists made me feel like it was happening again.' ∎

---

champion the trickle-down effect, environmental and cultural impacts are swept under the magic carpet of international travel. Labor issues, land rights and the reinforcing of colonial paradigms and stereotypes become invisible in the apparently unspoilt paradise inhabited by happy people waiting to service the needs of the well-traveled.

Small-scale, locally-owned and run tourism projects may create income for some local people. Even so, there may still be social, environmental and cultural downsides. To avoid these, and to maximize potential benefits, all sectors of the community need to be consulted about what form a particular tourism project should take. For the industry to help alleviate poverty,

---

Hurting the poor

Much of the world's multilateral development aid is channeled through international financial institutions (IFIs) such as the World Bank. Although the mission of most of these banks is poverty alleviation, many of their projects and policies have the reverse effect.

They provide subsidies to transnational corporations for investments around the world. These policies and practices generally hurt the poor; the revenues that are supposed to trickle down are often minimal, end up in the wrong pockets and do not compensate for negative social and environmental impacts.

Liberalization allows transnational corporations free rein to out-compete local and small scale businesses. ∎

---

local people need to have control of projects.

While the details of the processes of tourism 'development' vary from community to community, country to country and continent to continent, the dynamics remain essentially the same. Until the concerned traveling public vote with their feet and start to hold governments and TNCs to account for practices which destroy the very beauties, culture and specialness which they have come to see, the T&T industry will continue romping towards cultural homogenization and environmental destruction at the expense of the poorest and most vulnerable.

Tourism and the other WTO

For those who believe that tourism is just about lying on a beach, sightseeing, a little light shopping and chilling out, its inclusion on the agendas of the World

---

Tourist attractions

The tourist board of Chhattisgarh, India, pride themselves on their tribal (adivasi) population. The state actively reinforces the significance of the [adivasi] experience, promoting its, 'rich cultural heritage, the mystique of aboriginal tribal medicine, and attractive natural diversity'. Yet the day to day struggle of these communities is clearly at odds with this promotional spin.

Land is grabbed from the adivasis in numerous ways... in policies endorsed by the state and central governments. On a global scale, the West is willing to support and fund environmental, industrial and forest management projects whose benefits seldom filter down to the poor. ■

Action Village India.

Trade Organization (WTO), World Bank and IMF may seem puzzling. But its inclusion in the General Agreement on Trade in Services (GATS), signals the economic importance of this gigantic business sector.

Within the GATS, tourism is the most liberalized service sector with 125 of the WTO's 148 members undertaking commitments to progressively liberalize trade in travel and tourism related services. However, according to the Ecumenical Coalition on Tourism (ECOT), 'hasty liberalization of their tourism markets will sound a death knell for struggling developing economies keen to make economic gains through tourism... as the GATS supports large international corporations and not small local enterprises. Securing environmental and social regulation in tourism is close to impossible through the GATS as, by definition, it views tourism only through the narrow lens of trading opportunity'.[4]

And it is with the inclusion of tourism in the GATS that problems with lack of economic trickle-down are compounded and institutionalized. Like other WTO instruments, the GATS is negotiated by national governments through their trade delegations in Geneva. However, the GATS overrides any local jurisdictions, which means that if a local area or state's decision is incompatible with the national GATS commitments (highly possible, since local authorities are rarely consulted when national governments make commitments), the possibility arises that national governments would have to change locally evolved laws because they are WTO-incompatible.

Non-democratic tourism
This highlights the undemocratic way in which multilateral agreements are instated, with little regard for their impact on the most vulnerable communities. Lack of consultation, lack of transparency and a commitment to the largely Western TNCs' growth impacts on the lives of poor people affected by tourism. It also starts to answer the puzzling question of what happens to the money we spend on our holiday.

As Suresh comments, 'In the current negotiating climate, many governments are buckling under pressure [in GATS negotiations] by liberalizing 'harmless' sectors like tourism in the bargain to retain protection over more important sectors like agriculture. This trend heightens the need for governments to arrive at negotiating positions through an informed and consultative manner.'[4]

Tourism as consumerism
Like many apparent givens of Western consumer culture, the concept of tourism seems unquestioningly self-evident and apolitical. People work hard; they need to recharge their batteries so they go on holiday. But if hard work and battery recharging were the only elements of the equation we might reasonably expect paddy farmers, sweatshop workers and manual laborers from the Majority World to be exercising their democratic right to lounge on beaches, inspect ancient monuments and be waited on by cheerful natives of the industrial North. And although the middle classes of China and India are beginning to take up this form of consumerism, its political relations remain largely those of colonizers and colonized.

Because we're worth it
There are things humans have to consume, like food; then there are things that we were told we needed to consume, like cars; then there are the things we enjoy consuming just because we can, such as clothes, TV, travel and cultures. Despite pretensions to broaden the mind and the approving connotations of well-traveled, travel and tourism are political, social and economic choices disguised as consumption.

For whose benefit?
The UNWTO has produced a 10-point Global Code of Ethics for Tourism, featuring:
Article 1 Tourism's contribution to mutual understanding and respect between societies.
Article 2 Tourism as a vehicle for individual and collective fulfillment.
Article 7 Right to tourism.

Tourism as politics

The bias in terms of catering for the tourist is clear. What is unclear is how exactly tourism might contribute to the high-minded ideas expressed. Who has a 'right' to tourism? Not the guides, waiters or sarong-sellers of the Majority World, for whom getting a visa to travel to the North is well nigh impossible. And how does tourism provide individual and collective fulfillment for those shunted off their ancestral lands by an eco-tourism project or 5-star hotel complex?

As for contributing to mutual understanding and respect, what is the evidence for this? While some individuals may no doubt learn about other cultures and lifestyles as a result of their travels, it is a stretch of the imagination to suggest that interactions based primarily around a master/mistress and servant relationship will somehow transmute into a deeper understanding of the other person's way of life.

The bad news
Unlike the UNWTO, its sister agency, the United Nations Environment Program (UNEP) has actually researched the impact of tourism on host communities. Perhaps this is why it does not chunter on about poverty alleviation: 'The direct income for an area is the amount of tourist expenditure that remains locally

---

Suresh
A doctor, studying for a PhD in Oxford, Suresh comes from a well-connected family in Chennai, south India. 'Global tourism is an illusion created for and by people who want to do something because they can. It's more like an American way of life. If it's a 'dream' why question it? People work hard, they need rest and refreshment, so they have to tour! Why not? What physical work does a London desk-worker do? Well, there's a lot of mental stress so people could sleep more, spend more time with family and kids. But sometimes there's no relationship or no depth to the relationship, so we need more extras to pep up our lives to cover the apparent lack of quality. Is this what global tourism is for?' ■

after taxes, profits and wages are paid outside the area and after imports are purchased; these subtracted amounts are called leakage. In most all-inclusive package tours, about 80 per cent of travelers' expenditures go to the airlines, hotels and other international companies (who often have their headquarters in the travelers' home countries) and not to local businesses or workers.

'Of each $100 spent on a vacation tour by a tourist from a developed country, only around $5 actually stays in a developing country destination's economy.'

Some might argue that even though only a tiny proportion of the tourist spend will end up in the hands of the most needy, this something is better than nothing.

But it is at this point that the responsible traveler may start to ask how much they want to be part of such an exploitative and neo-colonial process. Questions could also be asked about why International Financial Institutions are so keen to finance tourism mega projects... and why governments are so keen to have them, despite all the associated problems. Small income-generation projects targeted at the poorest are the most effective at alleviating poverty. But of course these don't generate Forex or provide jobs for foreign businesses, consultancies and 'experts'.

Super-resorts

Like other Majority World governments, Sri Lanka's is keen on tourism. According to the Sri Lanka Development Forum 2005 papers, it is 'exploring all avenues to entice international hotel chains... Sheraton Group, Hyatt International and Ramada Group are planning to invest... The Ministry of Tourism is closely working with stakeholders to see the possibility of extending facilities to investors in the hotel industry and the recreational facility development areas.'

Under the heading: Transform Tourism to be a Foremost Foreign Exchange Generating Industry, the

---

Dangerous tourism

When a massive British-funded multi billion pound development was proposed in Zanzibar, [Tourism Concern] were approached by local people to question it on their behalf as it was too politically dangerous for them to do so. It could have been environmentally and socially disastrous – potentially displacing 20,000 local people, destroying the coral reefs and water supplies and preventing fishing communities from maintaining their livelihoods. ■

Tourism Concern, Campaigning for Change factsheet
www.tourismconcern.org.uk

---

report observes, 'For the tourism industry to suc-
ceed with sustainability it should generate revenue
on a par with other international businesses... The
Sri Lanka Tourist Board has already identified 24
Tourism Development Zones. There will be further
land acquisition and leasing of new areas for hotels
and recreational facility development...'

Post-tsunami land grab

For some, the southeast Asian tsunami of 2004 was a
disaster, but for the Sri Lanka Tourist board it was 'a
unique opportunity, and out of this tragedy will come
a world-class tourism destination'.[5]

In the wake of the catastrophe Sri Lanka has seen
massive grass-roots protests from local people who
have been excluded from consultation about redevel-
opment of tsunami-hit areas.

Plans are being developed to transform 15 coastal
towns into 'magnificent tourist resorts' under the
remit of a group headed by ten business leaders, five
of whom own or manage companies that operate
beach hotels. Local NGO coalition MONLAR is an
umbrella organization coordinating all the groups
opposing the official tsunami reconstruction plan.
'The rebuilding' says MONLAR, 'is completely counter to the interests of the people who have suffered in
the disaster.'[5]

So why do governments support these large-scale projects? They are financed by IFIs like the World Bank. According to Friends of the Earth International, direct financing of mega-projects like oil pipelines, gold mines and hydroelectric dams directly destroys environments and livelihoods. Cost overruns, displaced people, devastated environments and useless constructions are the unhappy results. Communities are deprived of access to natural resources. And the few jobs created cannot compensate for the livelihoods that are lost in the process.[3]

Is business politics?

Activist and writer Naomi Klein noted that: 'It is not just in the Majority World that catastrophe presents an opportunity for the corporate sector to "develop". Following the devastation wrought by Hurricane Katrina on the US city of New Orleans, Community Labor United, a coalition of low-income groups, issued the following statement. "The people of New Orleans will not go quietly into the night, scattering across this country to become homeless in other cities while federal relief funds are funneled into rebuilding casinos, hotels, chemical plants. We will not stand idly by while this disaster is used as an opportunity to replace our homes with newly built mansions and condos in a gentrified New Orleans". The group went on to demand that a committee made up of evacuees oversaw the Red Cross and other organizations collecting resources, and that evacuees "actively participate in the rebuilding..."'

However, not everyone was singing from the same hymn sheet. Jimmy Reiss, chair of the New Orleans Business Council, told Newsweek that he had been brainstorming about how 'to use this catastrophe as a once-in-an-eon opportunity to change the dynamic'. The Council's wish-list is said to include low wages, low taxes, more luxury condos and hotels.

Tourism as politics

Subsidizing tourism

As we have seen, governments are making decisions to support and subsidize T&T at the expense of other sectors which would more directly benefit their people. In 2005, the Tanzanian Government allocated $6 million to prop up its national carrier Air Tanzania Company Limited (ATC). Within the next two years it plans to give another $13m of taxpayers' money to the airline, known by locals as 'All Times Cancellation'.[6]

With many governments falling over themselves to generate foreign exchange at all costs by favoring tourism with tax breaks and the pick of desirable sites, tourism can be a political hot potato. It is a tribute to the power of the smoke and mirrors effect of this industry that tourists so often believe that they are in some way 'helping' local people achieve a better standard of living.

Bad politics

A funny thing happens (ie not a lot) when the T&T industry is called on to substantiate its fine words with action. Take for example, the continuing rhetoric from the WTTC, UNWTO and others on tourism's apparent ability to contribute to world peace.

The recent outbreak of hostilities which resulted in the Israeli regime raining bombs on civilian targets in Lebanon might have been an opportunity for T&T's movers and shakers to demonstrate to politicians exactly how to achieve world peace. Instead, even the industry-friendly eTurboNews (eTN) commented in July 2006 that 'unfortunately we have heard nothing from the "leaders" of the industry, despite tens of thousands of tourists in harm's way. Responses allude to the fact that we are in a state of war and that they do not want to get involved because it is "too political"'.[7]

A few days later, UNWTO managed the following powerful contribution to world peace: 'UNWTO shares the concerns of the world community, about the situation in Lebanon, Israel and the Palestinian territories, commiserates with grieving families and hopes for a speedy stabilization of the situation.' The press release then produced tourism statistics for the area, before continuing: 'The primary issue for our sector is the safety of tourists and their rapid repatriation from risk.'

Conspicuous by its absence is any concern for the local workers in the industry, let alone any allusions as to what exactly the tourism sector and UNWTO will be doing to create peace. Indeed, UNWTO Secretary-General Frangialli seems to have suffered a severe bout of amnesia about his previous 'tourism can contribute to world peace' comments. 'This is yet another example of where tourists and the industry are hostage to global events beyond their control...'

So if tourism doesn't contribute to world peace why does it say so often and so publicly that it does? It appears simply to be putting a positive gloss on the industry which without this figleaf might be revealed as something altogether less benign.

'Peace through tourism'?

Some time before, the International Institute for Peace through Tourism (IIPT) had claimed that it 'is dedicated to making travel and tourism the world's global peace industry.'[8]

Myths

The costs of tourism in a [Global South] country like India include extensive investment in fixed assets with a low rate of return for infrastructure, transportation, accommodation, cultural institutions, exhibition centers and park facilities. To this may be added the social and cultural costs like additional demands on infrastructure like land, water, health services; the creation of new jobs for displaced people; the cost of positive community relationships; the disparity between the lifestyle of visitors and those who serve them; the possible friction between local residents and new users of valued local resources; the perception of local residents of the spending of scarce capital resources on what they consider low priority areas like tourism; cultural costs of alterations in local ceremonial or traditional values; loss of privacy of local communities as tourists come to gape at their living conditions and rituals...

The tourism industry is generally self-centered and not given to educational, cultural or exchange programs on a philanthropic basis. Those questioning its impacts have to counter the myths of neo-classical economists in the field of tourism. ■

Nina Rao & KT Suresh, *Eco Tourism and Sustainable Development*, (Equations, Bangalore 1997).

IIPT president Louis J D'Amore said: 'IIPT... looks forward to collaborating in promoting travel throughout the world as a vital force in contributing to international understanding, cultural exchange, the reduction of poverty and preservation of biodiversity. It is only through travel and people-to-people encounters that we can come to realize the full significance of our inter-connectedness and common future in an ever shrinking 'Global Village'.'

Meanwhile, Frangialli, speaking in New York on the eve of the UN's Special General Assembly, asserted that '[Tourism] is a sector that promotes inter-cultural understanding and peace among nations.' However, this, apparently, is not exactly what he means (see box: 'UNWTO and world peace' on page 124).

No wonder tourists are confused. If any other sector: mining, oil, pharmaceuticals, agribusiness, textile manufacturing – came out with the same kind of rhetoric, more than a few eyebrows would be raised. Just what is so different about tourism? And if this is an industry genuinely motivated to create world peace or reduce poverty, why do we see so much talk and so little action?

Good politics
At another T&T industry meeting, the IMEX (the Worldwide Exhibition for Incentive Travel, Meetings and Events) Politicians' Forum, 'being too political' was presumably not a problem. The Forum 'welcomed politicians from Europe, as well as from Argentina, Georgia and Indonesia. After what was described as 'a full and productive day', Forum moderator, Michael Hirst, chair of the UK Business Tourism Partnership, told guests, 'You have now heard and seen why destinations that engender good working relations with their local politicians and develop a framework of support and promotion within an integrated municipal plan are those that are most successful.'[9]

Tourism as politics

British MP John Greenway pointed out that devolving responsibility for tourists and business tourism to the Mayor of London led to a much greater focus on promoting the City to various business markets. He said 'this is a stunning testimony to the Forum's theme of how political involvement can benefit the [travel] meetings industry.'

Lobbying
The industry's decision-makers systematically schmooze with politicians. In this way they lobby, influence and persuade them, without any counterbalancing input from groups pushing for other interests – for example protection of the environment or displaced communities. The inevitable result of this is to create a skewed tourism.

When combined with rhetoric about alleviating poverty and contributing to world peace this helps burnish further the halo that surrounds the industry.

New Tourism
In the New Tourism model, representatives of local groups who might be affected would be included in the consultations with decision-makers as a matter of course. It is, after all, astonishing that the sector has so much access to politicians while those most affected have virtually none. In an ideal world, it should be mandatory for civil society representatives to have both the access and the credibility to counter the claims of the industry to politicians at both a local and national level. Only in this way could a fair and non-exploitative model of tourism be created.

Supporting T&T
At the moment, tax breaks, reduced tariffs on imports, freezing of electricity and water rates, soft loans and other concessions encourage tourism development, although these fiscal incentives only benefit the

already affluent. When guides and souvenir-sellers cannot make ends meet through the off-season, they may have to turn to a money-lender, who may charge interest at 10 per cent per month. Those in most need of state support, especially in the absence of any form of social security, are left to fend for themselves.

Pro poor tourism

If governments were serious about using tourism to reduce poverty and create employment, the situation would be reversed – or at the very least, equalized. Souvenir-sellers, guides, rickshaw drivers and others would be given soft loans and, if necessary, mentored to build their business. Micro-credit and income-generating schemes for the off-season would be an essential part of the planning process. Training could be given in marketing, languages and other skills which local people decided they wanted.

Seminars could give local people a better under-standing of (Western) tourists and their lifestyles. Those selling goods and services around World Heritage Sites could be paid a retainer, or even a living wage. Why should all the money from cultural tourist attractions be siphoned away from the surrounding communities when it could make such a gigantic dif-ference to their lives?

Tourism as politics

In an effort to counteract problems like prostitution, alcoholism and drug use, which are often introduced or increased as a result of tourism, local groups could be developed to educate, inform and empower those affected (see more in chapter 7).

Locally led
These kinds of initiatives would be developed by local people, integrated with the cultural and social norms of an area, and be community-led rather than imposed by affluent urbanized élites.

Playing its part, the T&T industry might start lobbying for the introduction of these practices. Consultation with and representation of local people would be an accepted part of the process of tourism development.

Proactive tourists
However, for this to happen, there would need to be a turnaround in the way most governments approach

UNWTO and world peace

UNWTO Secretary-General Francesco Frangialli's special advisor (and past president of the World Travel and Tourism Council) Geoffrey Lipman clarifies the relationship between tourism and peace: 'It's a postulate. I don't think it was ever our intention to say our organization is helping to promote world peace. Tourism is an important factor in the peaceful development of society. In a post-conflict or post-disaster situation, one of the best ways to promote recovery in the region is the recovery of the tourism economy. I think we have a good case for saying that people to people interactions make a good case for peace. Economic development makes a good case for peace and the growth of tourism is important to both.

'Making it easier for people to travel is an important aspect of recovery generally and can be a contributory factor to peace. When people are easily able to move together and act in a responsible way, eg not going into mosques dressed in short skirts — it's helpful in contributing to lasting and enduring peace.'

Pressed to give concrete examples, Lipman cites Northern Ireland and post-war Europe, although he stresses, 'I'm not arguing in a particular case and a particular time. As a sector [tourism] is one of the contributors to harmonizing relationships with people. I'm not saying their people. If tourists lobbied foreign governments for these kinds of measures, this could provide additional motivation to make some of them happen.

Instead of merely bemoaning a fact that a local area has become 'spoilt', tourists could email their thoughts and comments to politicians, policymakers and CEOs. They could contact NGOs suggesting they campaign on these issues. If decision-makers found they were being called to account for their decisions, change could happen. We could lobby TV stations and other media to question their ethical stance. Boycotts of unethical products and operators could be organized. There are so many ways in which concerned members of the public can make their voices heard.

Local parliamentary reps could be asked for their position on a particular issue and encouraged to support a fairer system. People could also write to the embassies of relevant countries, praising or deploring particular initiatives, perhaps with the help of a petition.

---

that the UNWTO specifically makes it happen, but a lot goes on behind the scenes.'

According to Lipman, a lot went on behind the scenes in the Middle East six or seven years ago to create a framework for regional tourism. However, none of this 'people to people contact' has helped to create peace. Relating to the current conflict, he admits: 'There is not a tourist action agenda and to pretend there was would be to con you. You would be laughed at if you mentioned tourism.'

So tourism doesn't contribute to world peace? 'In the current situation you can't have specifics because it's not the time to have initiatives in tourism.' However: 'We did an interaction in North Korea – to build tourist bridges with South Korea. Anything that helps North Korea come into our society is a very good example of opening borders and minds. In Europe after the Second World War; the impact of tourism was a major factor in contributing to peace and stability.'

He continues, 'It's a very difficult thing to measure the absence of war then to cross-correlate it with a sector. I'm not saying we can show a demonstrable link, it's a postulate, with good anecdotal evidence. This is what our organization strongly believes. We're not missionaries; we're not trying to convert the world.' ∎

Tourism as politics

Will to act

As the Indian NGO Equations points out: 'We should not forget that tourism is an industry which emerges in the context of unresolved socio-economic structural issues, such as land distribution patterns or the take-over of traditional occupations by modern mechanized capital. Tourism happens to be a source of livelihood for millions... and aggressive privatization does not ensure social and economic safety nets. In the face of the unhindered entry of international capital and successive alienation, it is difficult to agree that, "the future is in our hands"'.

Those involved in, or with an interest in education, could challenge the neo-colonial myths still being perpetrated in subjects like geography and history. Those involved in the social sciences could examine the paradigm of superiority which is still a prevalent feature of many of the white races when dealing with those who are not white.

We need to recognize travel and tourism for what it is: part of a political process which benefits the most well-off, while, in many cases, making the lives of poor people more difficult. The next chapter looks at what we can do.

1 Koson Srisang, ed, 'Caught in Modern Slavery: Tourism and Child Prostitution in Asia', The Ecumenical Coalition on Third World Tourism, Bangkok 1991. **2** KT Suresh, 'Tourism Policy of India: an Exploratory Study', www.equitabletourism.org **3** Cited in 'Nature: poor people's wealth, Friends of the Earth International, July 2005 www.foei.org **4** KT Suresh, 'Democratizing Tourism!, ECOT, Hong Kong 2005. **5** 'Sri Lanka after the tsunami', In Focus, Tourism Concern, Summer 2005. www.tourismconcern.org **6** 'Taxpayers' money allocated to save ailing Tanzania's national airline', eTurboNews, 6.July 2006 www.eturbonews.com **7** 'Lebanon Crisis – what can the tourism industry do?', eTurboNews, 16 July 2006 **8** 'International Institute for Peace through Tourism signs on as sponsor for THETRADESHOW', eTN TravelPress, 14 July 2006. **9** 'IMEX Politicians Forum Report confirms success of new format and proof of grassroots progress', eTN TravelPress, 14 July 2006.

7 New tourism

Changing the operating practices of the global tourism industry is going to require more than a few 'eco' holidays and voluntary codes of practice. Here are some ways forward.

IT'S TIME TO challenge the way·the tourism industry operates. Throughout history there have been examples of practices that were seen as 'normal': women's subjugation; or supermarket dominance today, which have been examined and questioned, leading to the development of new paradigms and norms.

Economic globalization with the TNCs' stranglehold on the lives of billions has been scrutinized and found by many to be wanting. As a result, Fairtrade and organic brands have increased in popularity, while sweatshop labor in the global clothing industry has been exposed. The MakePovertyHistory coalition in the UK mobilized over 2 million people to protest about unfair trade rules, the iniquity of global poverty, HIV/AIDS and debt.

And in tourism there is the opportunity to challenge the doctrine of unrestricted consumerism at a personal and emotional level. As tourists, Northern citizens can see at first hand the impact of WTO, IMF and World Bank policies and initiatives on the people and environments of the global south. And as thinking people with a desire for fairness and equality, we can ask ourselves: do I want to be part of the problem, or part of the solution?

The personal is political
In the globalization context, we can be empowered visionaries actively involved in preserving and creating a better world, or we can be passive acceptors of the old exploitative model of human and planetary relationships.

Crushing complacency

Michael Willmot is co-founder of the Future Foundation, a market research think-tank, and one of the UK's leading futurologists. He believes that people's 'crushing complacency' is threatening our civilization. 'I believe the real threat is not coming from [voter] apathy but from our complacent, self-centered, self-satisfied view of the world.

'With so many choices and options open to so many individuals, certainly compared with earlier times, we have become complacent about our ambitions and about our consumer choices.'

Willmot explains: 'In my darker moments, I think "Is this the beginning of the end? Is this like Ancient Greece and Ancient Rome, where everybody became so self-obsessed and self-indulged that civilization collapses?"'

The solution, he reckons, is simple. 'We need to encourage the resurgence of research and we need to encourage the belief that we are all capable of analysis, so that people will come up with their own solutions to the problems they see around them.' ∎

'Why we can't be bothered to shake off complacency', *The Times*, 15 October 2005.

The global tourism industry needs a wake-up call. Western consumers are in an ideal position to put CEOs, governments and vested interests on notice that things have to change and that it's going to take something a lot more tangible than speeches about tourism 'alleviating poverty' or 'contributing to world peace' to convince us.

So many solutions

The discerning holiday consumer exists in many networks: work, family, social, interest groups, NGOs,

The New Tourist Code

We can all make a difference... if we want. Here are a few ideas.
● take as few trips as possible ● avoid flying as much as possible ● talk to local people as equals ● travel small-scale and lightly ● avoid package tours, hotel complexes, golf courses ● ask questions of the tour operator and local communities ● campaign ● question everything. ∎

political, spiritual and cultural groupings. Each and every one of these can be mobilized to create greater tourism justice. It's in the holidaymaker's best interest too. Can we really have a good time knowing that our visit is jeopardizing the very thing that we're enjoying? Surely we would prefer to be served by a waiter who is paid a decent wage which will support him and his family, rather than someone whose family skips meals because he doesn't earn enough to buy food.

We would all want the money which is daily siphoned out of Global South countries to be helping the guide who can't afford to pay hospital fees for his sick wife and baby, rather than pouring into the coffers of a global conglomerate so that its CEO can get a six figure bonus.

The aware tourist recognizes that there is more than a financial cost to their holiday and willingly accepts their responsibility in creating stewardship for the global commons, cultural, community and environmental.

Codes of conduct

In reality, an industry worth $600 billion a year, which employs 220 million people, and which is set to double in size in a decade, is not going to be effectively regulated or changed by a few unenforceable codes of conduct, no matter how worthy they sound. What is needed is stringent, far-reaching and enforceable

---

Hands tied

The driving force behind the GATS are those who stand to gain most: multinational corporations. As a country's obligations under GATS can supersede national, regional or local laws... local and national governments [have] their hands totally tied in terms of being able to decide how best to manage their economies, provide their public services and protect their environments. ...local government [is no longer] able to set limits on the size of hotels, or impose conditions on profit repatriation by foreign-owned tourism companies, or insist that local people are employed in management positions. This [is] as true for Hertfordshire as the Himalayas, the Alps or Antigua. Governments will... find strategic parts of their economies in the hands of multinational corporations and will have little recourse against them. ∎

Fair Trade in Tourism, Tourism Concern briefing document, 2003.

---

regulation. Tourism needs to be removed from the General Agreement on Trade in Services (GATS) and repositioned in the mind of the holidaying public as an industry which has more in common with say, mining, global agribusiness or textiles, than a harmless opportunity to soak up some sun and contribute in some vague way to a souvenir-seller's wellbeing by paying them a pittance.

Individuals – both within and outside the industry – interest groups and NGOs can campaign on this, giving real meaning to the rhetoric of the pro-globalization lobby. Joining or creating a group, or sending a letter or email to travel CEOs or political representatives (or both) is an excellent and worthwhile first step.

Fair trade in tourism

In contrast to voluntary codes of conduct which are not worth the paper they're written on – except as a means of persuading the unwitting that 'something' is being done, and that business can carry on as usual – we need to see a sea change in the attitude of the holidaymaking public, those within the T&T industry itself, and governments at both a local and national level.

However, we cannot assume that all or even most holidaymakers will welcome challenges to their apparent 'right' to a holiday, regardless of environmental cost and social justice. Travel journalist Alison Rice speaks for many when she says that 'too many of us work too many hours for too many weeks of the year not to want our holidays to be perfect. We need our hard-earned, tax-paid, disposable cash to deliver us a break away from every niggle of everyday life. In the words of the MD of a major package holiday company, "Holidays have to deliver a continual stream of perfect moments."'[1]

Alison Rice's straight from the hip honesty (see 'Perfect moments' box) reveals the reality of deeply embedded attitudes among the holidaymaking public

---

'Perfect moments'

A fair percentage of readers/listeners/viewers... tell me that their brush with 'local people' adds much to their holidays. A tale to tell of visiting a local school, catching a wedding, chatting about football is a souvenir more special than a suntan or a T-shirt. But spending time in someone else's home, coping with different quality standards, language barriers and unfamiliar manners do not deliver most people's perfect moments.

At home we are always tackling uncomfortable stuff, be it TV coverage of war/famine/disasters or our own local community issues, schooling perhaps, or transport or crime. No wonder every year we strive for a fortnight of perfect moments. If a family gains maximum enjoyment from wallowing in a marble-clad hotel with like-minded people and satellite TV and barbecued hamburgers, who gains what if they sacrifice their perfect moments for the uncomfortable experience of being polite to strangers in unaccustomed surroundings?

Who gains what if I swap the relaxed brandy, cigars and chat for local hooch, a rough bed and strained interaction that makes me fretful with all that white liberal guilt?

For 50 weeks of every year, I'm prepared to be anxious about the unfairness of global trade. I'll campaign, I'll send cheques. But please, let me have two weeks stuffed with my very own perfect moments. ■

Alison Rice, *Fair Trade in Tourism*, Tourism Concern Fair Trade in Tourism Network, issue 4 Autumn 2002.

Travel and tourism media code of conduct

Travel journalists can do much more to champion the rights of poor people – see the hints and tips below.

● report on negative impacts of holidays on hosts, environment, culture ● stop promoting overseas weekend away trips ● suggest that travelers fly less ● accurately report tourist impacts on host communities ● stop accepting travel freebies from travel companies ● become truly independent and impartial reporters, rather than the marketing arm of the tourism industry ● lobby the industry about their human rights, labor and environmental records ● question the assumption that promoting luxurious colonial-style holidays in the Global South is acceptable ● challenge the notion that global tourism is fine for the citizens of rich northern countries, while people from the Global South are routinely discriminated against, in everything from visa applications to international passport control ● act as if traveling to another country was an incredible privilege – not another notch on the tourism consumer's belt. ■

which are strikingly at odds with the rhetoric of how 'meeting the locals' and 'people-to-people contact' contribute to global peace, the phrases favored by the marketing departments of global T&T.

Imperfect moments?

And of course, there is a cost. Rice's (and other holidaymakers') perfect moments will be paid for by people, living at or near the poverty line; environments which are being systematically destroyed, and cultures and customs which are being commoditized and turned into museum pieces. Other costs in the who gains what dilemma are: children dying of malnutrition, illiteracy, lives shortened and made more painful than they need be because of lack of access to medical services. All of these could benefit from fairly traded, just and equitable tourism practices.

Media moments

The mainstream media is all too often a happy collaborator with the global T&T industry, promoting it as a fun activity, where the only serious questions asked are about value for money and the state of play of hotel rooms and other facilities for the tourist. Bringing out the occasional supplement on 'green' tourism or 'eco' lodges without addressing the wider issues and ramifications of this global extractive industry may have been good enough in the dark ages, but in the 21st century, it's simply lazy and unacceptable journalism.

Travel journalists and other media professionals need to take on board that unfettered industrial tourism has the potential to destroy communities, livelihoods and fragile environments, and acknowledge that the world is more than a gigantic theme park in which the privileged kidults of rich northern countries can play.

We need more investigative media stories on the truth behind the 'smiling faces' façade. And how about – heaven forefend – interviews and jolly little 'my life in travel' style pieces from waiters, guides and sarong-sellers telling the other side of the holiday paradise story?

Tourism justice

Human rights are just as much part of the tourism industry as they are of any other part of life. One way in which they can be protected and enhanced is by fairly traded and ethical tourism, using a model based on the terms of reference of the Fairtrade Labelling Organization (FLO).

Just say 'no'

ECOT's (Ecumenical Coalition on Tourism) vision of tourism... is one wherein people enrich their lives in encounters that safeguard the dignity of every person, respect diverse cultural heritages, protect and promote the Earth's integrity and thus foster harmony and peace. ECOT supports and advances the idea of less self-indulgent and self-centered visitations and seeks to promote more self-conscious tourism including the right of the visited to say 'no' to tourism. ∎

Democratizing Tourism! ECOT, March 2005.

New tourism

In stark contrast to the woolly and aspirational prose of the UNWTO, WTTC et al, FLO's feasibility study on Fairtrade-labeled tourism (FLT) due to be completed in September 2006, is a model of specificity, timelines, stakeholder engagement and deliverables.

Specific issues to be addressed include: the product; the target group (of beneficiaries); FT pricing; long-term relationships; segments of supply chains to be certified; scope of the labeling; environmental concerns; and the relationship of FTL tourism with private/public, governmental and non-governmental efforts. The relationship of how FTL brings an added value to communities is specifically mentioned, as is how it could work with initiatives developed by UNESCO, UNEP and UNWTO. Marketing and strategies, as well as consumer and producer awareness are also included in the model.[2]

Guidelines

The FLO feasibility study is an object lesson in how to research and define terms; investigate markets; target, implement and structure pricing so as to ensure that target groups benefit. Supply chain linkages, the trading structure of the mainstream market, the way in which the social premium might be handled transparently, and the way in which ethical standards of employment and trade can be ensured in the South

---

Tormented tripper

The Seychelles – a massively deceptive place. The name conjures idyllic and tranquil images when in reality it's a dictatorship where people are suffering. If you venture off the beaten track you see animals being treated appallingly. I was really tormented by it.

Terracotta travels

I want to see the Terracotta Warriors in China. The human-rights issue doesn't appeal, but I would like to discover the country's history. ■

Greg Lake, 'Independent Traveller', *The Independent*, 5 August 2006.

are all considered. A separate section outlines the consultation process, including groups, organizations and individuals consulted.

All of this could be incorporated into normal trading practice, were there the will, of any or all T&T operators. It's not rocket science, it's about putting corporate money where the corporate marketing speak and toothless Corporate Social Responsibility rhetoric are.

One way in which concerned holidaymakers can prod the T&T industry to benefit the least well off, is to lobby its representatives – tour operators, internet booking agencies, airlines and anyone they come across in the process of choosing and booking a flight or holiday, for information on pay and conditions, local benefits, environmental protection and sustainability.

Write letters, send emails, organize petitions; become empowered. Demand that the industry adopt the principles and practicalities of Fair Trade, not as an opportunistic PR marketing exercise, but as a genuine, far-reaching and visionary response to the reality of our global interconnectedness.

As one Egyptian Fair Trade in Tourism network partner, Sherif Al-Ghamrawy, has pointed out: 'If even one per cent of the tourists who came to Egypt decided they wanted this sort of tourism, it would transform our lives and our country'.[3]

The dangers of ecotourism 'lite'

Clearly the travel industry has an interest in promoting the world's natural and cultural resources, which are at the core of its business activities. But it has other concerns as well, some of which run counter to the tenets of sound ecotourism. Travel associations advocate... self-regulation, expanded tourism markets and a lowering of trade barriers. [They have] responded to the growth of environmental concerns and the rise of ecotourism by instituting certain changes that... often amount to promoting minor, cost-saving environmental reforms – ecotourism 'lite' - rather than seriously grappling with the principles and practices of ecotourism.

Much of what is marketed as ecotourism is simply conventional mass tourism wrapped in a thin veneer of green. Ecotourism lite is propelled by travel agents, tour operators, airlines and cruise lines, large hotels and resort chains and international organizations which promote quick, superficially 'green' visits within conventional packages.

Ecotourism lite travelers are 'entertained by nature, but not unduly concerned with its preservation'. The ultimate goal of ecotourism should be to infuse the whole travel industry with the principles and practices of ecotourism. There is some movement in that direction on the part of many travelers but the movement towards ecotourism lite, towards industry 'greenwashing' through advertising images and cosmetic changes is stronger. When poorly planned, unregulated and overhyped, ecotourism lite – like mass tourism, or even traditional nature tourism – can bring only marginal financial benefits but serious environmental and social consequences.

A walk through the rainforest is not ecotourism unless that particular walk somehow benefits that environment and the people who live there. A rafting trip is only ecotourism if it raises awareness and helps protect the watershed. A loose interpretation allows many companies to promote themselves as something they are not. If true ecotourism is important to you, ask plenty of questions: is the environment being cared for? Is there genuine effort to help the local economies? Are resources being left intact for future generations? Is the local culture being honored and valued and not just photographed? These questions will cut through the semantics and allow you to see what is really being offered. ∎

Mike Merg, 'The Greenwashing of the Travel Industry', January 2005. www.untamedpath.com

Willing to pay more

According to Tourism Concern, research commissioned by the Association of British Travel Agents

(ABTA) found that two thirds of package tourists questioned said they would be happy to pay an extra £10-25/$20-50 towards environmental or social improvements. Research by Mintel in 2001 showed that 28 per cent of respondents understood that tourism can ruin local culture, while 27 per cent have seen something on holiday which disturbed them, such as poverty or beach erosion, and a quarter are concerned about the local environment.[3]

Many of us will understand where Greg Lake is coming from (see box, 'Tormented tripper' p134). But we simply can't switch off global realities in order to justify what we want to do. Many people love the concept of the 'global village' when it means fusion foods and holiday breaks in the Seychelles and China. But can we switch off our integrity, values and conscience to support regimes and ways of doing things which in any context other than our own holiday we may well find morally repugnant?

Initiatives such as Fair Trade labeling in tourism

A doctor's view

'If people were not working in the tourist sector, they would be agriculturalists, doing laundry, being butchers, being human transport or probably doing some other backbreaking job in the manufacturing sector, although these are being eliminated by mechanization. If they did these sort of jobs instead of working in tourism, the work is harder but at least they would be working for a local owner, and on their own land. That matters because workers can rebel or strike, but it's an internal problem. The ownership and profits stay in that country and may be of use to future generations.

But in today's TNC-run tourism industry, there's no real owner, just a bundle of wealthy investors who continuously skim profits. There's no way an islander in, say, the Seychelles, can in the future control the Hilton Group [mainly hotels], or ever have access to the profits...

Tourism is just one way in which the greedy élite profit from the poor and make them more poor. There needs to be a complete overhaul of the way the global economic system is run. Small measures will do no good.' ■

Dr Suresh Munuswamy, healthcare professional, Chennai, India.

are only part of the potential solution to a large and complex problem. The inequities of global trade rules skewed to benefit TNCs and the populations of the rich countries need to be challenged.

Rhetoric or reality?
One of the questions facing the holidaymaker when selecting a holiday is how to figure out whether it really does what it says on the label. What is a 'green' holiday? Is ecotourism good for the environment and local people? And how can an industry predicted to almost double in size in 10 years, gobbling up cultures, environments and communities, ever suggest that it's sustainable?

New Tourism suggests that we need to take a long, hard look at some of the concepts bandied about by industry TNCs to discover just how much truth there is in their self-serving assertions.

Questions
As Mike Merg demonstrates (see box on 'Ecotourism lite' p 136), questions are the way forward when it comes to individuals and campaigning organizations making inroads into changing practices within the global T&T industry.

Aware tourists will look both ways when investigating the reality of their holiday. One direction will be to question and hold to account their tour operator, hotelier and airline; the other will question their hosts, based on a genuine desire to learn about another way of life, including how local people are affected.

Those paddy fields again
One of the ways in which almost everyone involved in T&T, from the loftiest CEO in his air-conditioned office, to the souvenir-seller tramping up and down a baking beach, to the tourist swigging beer and eating prawns, will agree, is that 'people are better off

working in tourism rather than in the paddy fields'.

Note, it is always the paddy fields. Not coal mines or garages. Not working in a hospital, as a fisherperson, or a farmer with a small-holding. Not having a small shop, or being a teacher, or a factory worker.

It's almost as though certain chunks of the global population are given only one choice: do you want to work in the grindingly hard and uncertain but at least regular (though low-status) work of your ancestors, with little or no prospects of betterment, where you will run the risk of snakebites and scorpion attacks on daily basis?

Or do you want to leave your village and support network to chance your luck as a waiter or room-cleaner, where you may well be lonely and exposed to cultural influences which will probably undermine your previous way of life? You may be dazzled by the possibility of making (you believe) substantial amounts of cash from rich foreigners by doing 'clean', 'easy' work. You may acquire an air of modern sophistication to impress the folks back home. You may acquire habits of drink and drug-dependence, and social anomie; you may develop a sense of poverty and cultural inferiority.

So maybe there's no real choice, just people trying to get by. But seeing work in the paddy fields as the ONLY alternative to working in tourism is simplistic. If the millions of dollars pumped into large-scale tourism projects were redirected in smaller, community-led initiatives targeted at poverty alleviation, environmental protection and the preservation of fragile cultures, a myriad of real choices would open up.

We have seen that the tourism industry is part and parcel of an unjust global economic system. Its exploitation of the poor and the environment is not going to halt overnight. It is not just a simple question of 'being nice to local residents', collecting toilet paper from the Annapurna Trail, or organizing a group of horse-riders, scooter-riders, cyclists or bungee jumpers to have a lovely holiday while raising money for charity. And it is definitely not about TNCs appropriating the language of empowerment and equity at conferences, in press releases and on websites, while continuing to run businesses which create poverty and degrade and devastate the environment.

The points made by ActionAid (see box 'Power politics') are just as relevant to other global industries. Harry Goodman, the man behind Intersun and Air Europe, the model of all charter airlines said he knew his charter-flight holidays in the 1970s put too much pressure on the infrastructure of his [sic] destinations; he continued because no one told him to stop.[4]

Change is always possible, but it takes motivation. Personal motivation depends on many factors and there is a very real sense in which large segments of the populations in rich countries have informally

---

Power politics

Unequal and unjust power relations lie at the root of poverty. Unequal power relationships are systematically imposed in both poor and rich countries on the basis of gender, age, caste, class, ethnicity... race and disability. All too often, powerful vested interests – communities, institutions, corporations and nations – choose to exercise the power they have, in order to accumulate more power. They abdicate their obligations by denying rights, resources and opportunities to the less fortunate, particularly to the poor and excluded.

Lack of power is inextricably tied to the denial of basic human rights. Rights are denied at local, international and international level, as power imbalances between rich and poor countries play out in policies which hurt poor and excluded people.

Double standards and gross power imbalances are evident in the working of international institutions, the actions of governments and the power of global corporations.

Change will only come through people organizing for their rights and working to redistribute power within and between communities and nations. Poor and excluded people cannot do it alone. A global wave of citizen action holds far-reaching potential. The history of corporate social responsibility has shown that voluntary initiatives have limited impact and that greater regulation is now needed. ∎

'Rights to end poverty', ActionAid UK strategy 2005-2010.

absolved themselves from taking responsibility for the consequences of their actions.

Many of us have engaged so deeply and fervently with the currently model of lifestyle consumerism that we are blinded to the possibility that life can be organized in any other way. Rather than seeking out ways to challenge what is, after all, a comparatively new model of human relationships – that money, consumerism and individual gratification have primacy over all other values – we have mortgaged our hearts, conscience and time to the all-powerful deity of Mammon.

Like journalist Alison Rice, we may feel that we are 'dealing with' war, famine, terrorism on a daily basis by watching the TV or reading the newspapers. But this is observing, probably with a large element of denial. It is not 'dealing with' the issues unless we take action to challenge the status quo which enables such outrages to continue day after day, year after year. By inaction we give the warmongers, the vested political and corporate interests carte blanche to continue wreaking havoc on the poor and the planet.

In many ways, global tourism is the last bastion of a world dedicated to increasing the benefits for the rich to the increasing detriment of the poor. Until we as the traveling public say, enough is enough; until we demand real change in this gigantic politico-industrial sector; until we truly accept that our holidays are in their homes and recognize the implications of this; we will continue to exploit and destroy fragile and finite environments; irreplaceable cultural traditions; and promote inequality and exploitation whenever we go on holiday. The solutions are in our hands.

1 Alison Rice, 'Community interaction is important to me on holiday,' *Fair Trade in Tourism*, Tourism Concern, Issue 4, Autumn 2002. **2** Terms of Reference, feasibility study on Fairtrade-labelled tourism, Fairtrade Labelling Organizations International, Bonn, June 2006. **3** *Fair Trade in Tourism*, briefing document, Tourism Concern 2003. **4** Tim Forsyth, 'Sustainable Tourism: Moving from Theory to Practice', WWF-UK, 1996.

Contacts

INTERNATIONAL

ActionAid India
C-88 ND SEII
New Delhi 110049
Tel: + 91 11 41640571-76
www.actionaidindia.org

Equations
415 2-C Cross, 4th Main Road
OMBR Layout Banaswadi
Bangalore 560043 INDIA
Tel: +91 80 25457607/25457659
fax: +91 80 25457665
www.equitabletourism.org
info@equitabletourism.org

Friends of the Earth International
PO Box 19199
1000 GD Amsterdam
Netherlands
Tel: +31 20 22 1369
Fax: +31 20 639 2181
www.foei.org

MONLAR (Movement for National Land and Agricultural Reform)
1151/58A, 4th Lane, Kotte Road
Rajagiriya
Sri Lanka
Tel: +94 11 286 5534
Fax: +94 11 440 7663
monlar@sltnet.lk

NEW ZEALAND/ AOTEAROA

ECPAT NZ Inc
www.ecpat.org.nz

AUSTRALIA

Ecotourism Resource Centre
www.bigvolcano.com.au/ercentre

CANADA

Green Tourism Association
info@greentourism.ca

Tourism Information Network
webhome.idirect.com/-tourism

UK

ActionAid
Website: www.actionaid.org

Action Village India
www.actionvillageindia.org.uk

ECPAT UK
info@ecpat.org.uk
www.ecpat.org.uk

Tourism Concern
www.tourismconcern.org.uk

Traidcraft
Meet the People Tours are organized and managed by Saddle Skedaddle Ltd on behalf of Traidcraft.
traidcraft@skedaddle.co.uk

US

Ecotour at Conservation International
www.conservation.org

Index

Index